Approaches to learning and teaching

English as a Second Language

a toolkit for international teachers

Margaret Cooze

Series Editors: Paul Ellis and Lauren Harris

CAMBRIDGE
UNIVERSITY PRESS

University Printing House, Cambridge CB2 8BS, United Kingdom

One Liberty Plaza, 20th Floor, New York, NY 10006, USA

477 Williamstown Road, Port Melbourne, VIC 3207, Australia

4843/24, 2nd Floor, Ansari Road, Daryaganj, Delhi – 110002, India

79 Anson Road, #06–04/06, Singapore 079906

Cambridge University Press is part of the University of Cambridge.

It furthers the University's mission by disseminating knowledge in the pursuit of education, learning and research at the highest international levels of excellence.

www.cambridge.org
Information on this title: www.cambridge.org/9781316639009 (Paperback)

© Cambridge International Examinations 2017

First published 2017

20 19 18 17 16 15 14 13 12 11 10 9 8 7 6 5 4 3 2 1

Printed in Great Britain by CPI Group (UK) Ltd, Croydon CR0 4YY

A catalogue record for this publication is available from the British Library

ISBN 978-1-316-63900-9 Paperback

Contents

Acknowledgements

The authors and publishers acknowledge the following sources of copyright material and are grateful for the permissions granted.

Cover bgblue/Getty Images; Fig 9.4 screenshot from the English Vocabulary Profile (www.englishprofile.org) © Cambridge University Press; Fig 10.1 is used by kind permission of Crossbow Education Ltd; Fig 10.2 Hero Images/Getty Images; Online Lesson idea 3.1 david franklin/Getty Images; Kyle Werstiuk/Getty Images; Boy_Anupong/ Getty Images; jackie cooper/Getty Images; Online Lesson idea 4.4 Westend61/Getty Images; Jade Brookbank/Getty Images; Martin Ward/ Getty Images; Sanchai Khudpin/Shutterstock; Glenn Van Der Knijff/ Getty Images; Lesson idea 6.3 PM Images/Getty Images, Caiaimage/ Chris Ryan/Getty Images, David Schaffer/Getty Images

All other photos within online lesson ideas are © Margaret Cooze

Introduction to the series by the editors

1

1 Approaches to learning and teaching English as a Second Language

This series of books is the result of close collaboration between Cambridge University Press and Cambridge International Examinations, both departments of the University of Cambridge. The books are intended as a companion guide for teachers, to supplement your learning and provide you with extra resources for the lessons you are planning. Their focus is deliberately not syllabus-specific, although occasional reference has been made to programmes and qualifications. We want to invite you to set aside for a while assessment objectives and grading, and take the opportunity instead to look in more depth at how you teach your subject and how you motivate and engage with your students.

The themes presented in these books are informed by evidence-based research into what works to improve students' learning and pedagogical best practices. To ensure that these books are first and foremost practical resources, we have chosen not to include too many academic references, but we have provided some suggestions for further reading.

We have further enhanced the books by asking the authors to create accompanying lesson ideas. These are described in the text and can be found in a dedicated space online. We hope the books will become a dynamic and valid representation of what is happening now in learning and teaching in the context in which you work.

Our organisations also offer a wide range of professional development opportunities for teachers. These range from syllabus- and topic-specific workshops and large-scale conferences to suites of accredited qualifications for teachers and school leaders. Our aim is to provide you with valuable support, to build communities and networks, and to help you both enrich your own teaching methodology and evaluate its impact on your students.

Each of the books in this series follows a similar structure. In the first chapter, we have asked our authors to consider the essential elements of their subject, the main concepts that might be covered in a school curriculum, and why these are important. The next chapter gives you a brief guide on how to interpret a syllabus or subject guide, and how to plan a programme of study. The authors will encourage you to think too about what is not contained in a syllabus and how you can pass on your own passion for the subject you teach.

The main body of the text takes you through those aspects of learning and teaching which are widely recognised as important. We would like to stress that there is no single recipe for excellent teaching, and that different schools, operating in different countries and cultures, will have strong traditions that should be respected. There is a growing consensus, however, about some important practices and approaches that need to be adopted if students are going to fulfil their potential and be prepared for modern life.

In the common introduction to each of these chapters we look at what the research says and the benefits and challenges of particular approaches. Each author then focuses on how to translate theory into practice in the context of their subject, offering practical lesson ideas and teacher tips. These chapters are not mutually exclusive but can be read independently of each other and in whichever order suits you best. They form a coherent whole but are presented in such a way that you can dip into the book when and where it is most convenient for you to do so.

The final two chapters are common to all the books in this series and are not written by the subject authors. Schools and educational organisations are increasingly interested in the impact that classroom practice has on student outcomes. We have therefore included an exploration of this topic and some practical advice on how to evaluate the success of the learning opportunities you are providing for your students. The book then closes with some guidance on how to reflect on your teaching and some avenues you might explore to develop your own professional learning.

We hope you find these books accessible and useful. We have tried to make them conversational in tone so you feel we are sharing good practice rather than directing it. Above all, we hope that the books will inspire you and enable you to think in more depth about how you teach and how your students learn.

Paul Ellis and Lauren Harris

Series Editors

2 | Purpose and context

International research into educational effectiveness tells us that student achievement is influenced most by what teachers do in classrooms. In a world of rankings and league tables we tend to notice performance, not preparation, yet the product of education is more than just examinations and certification. Education is also about the formation of effective learning habits that are crucial for success within and beyond the taught curriculum.

The purpose of this series of books is to inspire you as a teacher to reflect on your practice, try new approaches and better understand how to help your students learn. We aim to help you develop your teaching so that your students are prepared for the next level of their education as well as life in the modern world.

This book will encourage you to examine the processes of learning and teaching, not just the outcomes. We will explore a variety of teaching strategies to enable you to select which is most appropriate for your students and the context in which you teach. When you are making your choice, involve your students: all the ideas presented in this book will work best if you engage your students, listen to what they have to say, and consistently evaluate their needs.

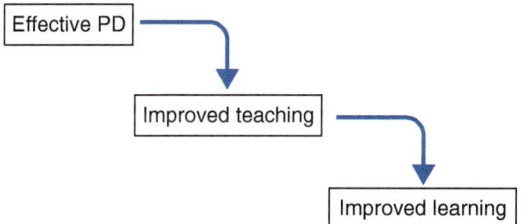

Cognitive psychologists, coaches and sports writers have noted how the aggregation of small changes can lead to success at the highest level. As teachers, we can help our students make marginal gains by guiding them in their learning, encouraging them to think and talk about how they are learning, and giving them the tools to monitor their success. If you take care of the learning, the performance will take care of itself.

When approaching an activity for the first time, or revisiting an area of learning, ask yourself if your students know how to:

- approach a new task and plan which strategies they will use
- monitor their progress and adapt their approach if necessary
- look back and reflect on how well they did and what they might do differently next time.

Effective learners understand that learning is an active process. We need to challenge and stretch our students and enable them to interrogate, analyse and evaluate what they see and hear. Consider whether your students:

- challenge assumptions and ask questions
- try new ideas and take intellectual risks
- devise strategies to overcome any barriers to their learning that they encounter.

As we discuss in the chapters on **Active learning** and **Metacognition**, it is our role as teachers to encourage these practices with our students so that they become established routines. We can help students review their own progress as well as getting a snapshot ourselves of how far they are progressing by using some of the methods we explore in the chapter on **Assessment for Learning**.

Students often view the subject lessons they are attending as separate from each other, but they can gain a great deal if we encourage them to take a more holistic appreciation of what they are learning. This requires not only understanding how various concepts in a subject fit together, but also how to make connections between different areas of knowledge and how to transfer skills from one discipline to another. As our students successfully integrate disciplinary knowledge, they are better able to solve complex problems, generate new ideas and interpret the world around them.

In order for students to construct an understanding of the world and their significance in it, we need to lead students into thinking habitually about why a topic is important on a personal, local and global scale. Do they realise the implications of what they are learning and what they do with their knowledge and skills, not only for themselves but also for their neighbours and the wider world? To what extent can they recognise and express their own perspective as well as the perspectives of others? We will consider how to foster local and global awareness, as well as personal and social responsibility, in the chapter on **Global thinking**.

As part of the learning process, some students will discover barriers to their learning: we need to recognise these and help students to overcome them. Even students who regularly meet success face their own challenges. We have all experienced barriers to our own learning at some point in our lives and should be able as teachers to empathise and share our own methods for dealing with these. In the chapter on **Inclusive education** we discuss how to make learning accessible for everyone and how to ensure that all students receive the instruction and support they need to succeed as learners.

Some students are learning through the medium of English when it is not their first language, while others may struggle to understand subject jargon even if they might otherwise appear fluent. For all students, whether they are learning through their first language or an additional language, language is a vehicle for learning. It is through language that students access the content of the lesson and communicate their ideas. So, as teachers, it is our responsibility to make sure that language isn't a barrier to learning. In the chapter on **Language awareness** we look at how teachers can pay closer attention to language to ensure that all students can access the content of a lesson.

Alongside a greater understanding of what works in education and why, we as teachers can also seek to improve how we teach and expand the tools we have at our disposal. For this reason, we have included a chapter in this book on **Teaching with digital technologies**, discussing what this means for our classrooms and for us as teachers. Institutes of higher education and employers want to work with students who are effective communicators and who are information literate. Technology brings both advantages and challenges and we invite you to reflect on how to use it appropriately.

This book has been written to help you think harder about the impact of your teaching on your students' learning. It is up to you to set an example for your students and to provide them with opportunities to celebrate success, learn from failure and, ultimately, to succeed.

We hope you will share what you gain from this book with other teachers and that you will be inspired by the ideas that are presented here. We hope that you will encourage your school leaders to foster a positive environment that allows both you and your students to meet with success and to learn from mistakes when success is not immediate. We hope too that this book can help in the creation and continuation of a culture where learning and teaching are valued and through which we can discover together what works best for each and every one of our students.

3 | The nature of
the subject

Why English?

We are in a privileged position as teachers of English. The language will most likely play an important part in the lives of our students and so our role is vital. English is an international language and is used by millions of people all over the world for study, pleasure and business. Our students might be more interested in using English to watch films, listen to music or access social media on the internet. All of these areas are important, and we know that language learning helps students in other subjects too. It aids cognitive development and helps our students to be creative. There are also many transferable skills, for example communicating effectively and analysing things. Second language students often carry this back to their first language, making them better first language users, too. Ellen Bialystok, a psychologist at York University in Toronto, carried out research which showed that being bilingual can even help to prevent some of the diseases that people develop in later life, such as dementia.

Students about to leave school soon realise that there are exciting opportunities for English speakers. This usually means that our students are very motivated. It's our job to use this motivation to make sure they can do their very best.

What is English for you?

English has grown in importance over the past few decades and I'm sure this won't change. More students are learning English at primary school now but most students really start to focus on English at secondary school. As English teachers, we have a responsibility to our students to provide them with interesting, relevant lessons that are also fun.

Some of us will be teaching English as a stand-alone subject. It may be a second language, but could be a third language if you work in a plurilingual situation. Or you may be teaching in a school where English is used to teach other subjects, such as mathematics or history. We'll talk about that more in Chapter 9. We all know, however, that whatever situation we are teaching in, to teach well we need to consider some key areas.

What are we teaching?

The most obvious answer to this question is … language! But what do we mean by that? Probably, we mean structure and grammar, vocabulary and pronunciation. We'll look at what it means to teach these later in the book.

Something that is less obvious is teaching our students *when* they should use certain language. This may be because they need to think about who they are talking to and how formal or informal the situation is. But it can also be because certain language doesn't 'fit' in certain situations. It could be a matter of collocation with vocabulary: for example, we say a 'generation gap', but not a 'generation space' (although *gap* and *space* have similar meanings). Or maybe it's using formal language in an informal setting, which might sound odd.

Typically, grammar and vocabulary are presented in a context or a situation that shows the meaning. If students see or hear the language in a context, it helps them to understand and remember more easily. For example, explaining the word 'exhausted' is more difficult than showing the meaning in a text on marathon runners. Students work out new grammar and vocabulary in their first language using the context they see it in – usually without thinking about what they are doing. However, they don't always use the same skills in a second language and we need to teach them how to do this.

Each skill can be broken down into a number of sub-skills. For example, with reading, some sub-skills are:

- reading for gist (skim reading)
- reading for specific information (scan reading)
- reading for detail
- deducing meaning from context
- understanding text structure.

▣ LESSON IDEA ONLINE 3.1: AN AUSTRALIAN CITY
This reading comprehension activity provides practice in different reading sub-skills as well as opportunities for speaking practice. Which of the reading sub-skills mentioned above are used in this activity?

Our students use these sub–skills subconsciously in their first language, but we need to help them to recognise these skills in English, too. We rarely use one skill on its own. In true communication most skills are integrated with each other. If we read a book, we might talk about it with friends or write about it in an email to someone. It would be very strange not to think about the two skills of speaking and listening together – they are fundamentally interlinked.

Teacher Tip

The next time you have a listening text with questions in your coursebook, split the class into two groups. Then:

- Copy the odd-numbered questions onto a separate sheet for half the class.
- Give the even-numbered questions to the other half of the class.
- Ask students to answer their questions as they listen.
- Ask them to find a partner from the other group to discuss their questions and answers. This creates an opportunity to combine their listening and speaking skills in one activity.

Who are we teaching?

My teaching changes depending on the characteristics of my students. Younger children often have less fear of making mistakes, which is great, but they also have shorter attention spans, which isn't always as useful. Older students are able to take more control of their own learning and can think in more abstract ways. Different students have different interests and ways of learning so it is important to make sure that our lesson content is as relevant and suitable as possible. The content and pace of lessons will differ between these two groups. Even if you teach one age group, no two classes are ever the same!

Teacher Tip

Think of a lesson you taught recently. How would you change it for a different age group?

For example, you might have a reading text that is suitable for different age groups but that is too long for younger students. You could rewrite it to make it shorter, but this might mean it loses some of its meaning. An alternative would be to break the text down into chunks and after each chunk have a comprehension activity or discussion. This introduces a change of focus, which keeps younger students' attention for longer.

How are we teaching?

In Chapter 4 we'll talk about the various approaches to teaching that different teachers take, for example grammar translation, a lexical approach or a communicative approach. I think most of us nowadays take the best bits from each approach and use them to fit our lessons. Sometimes it's important to focus on functional language such as 'asking for permission' or 'explaining a process' and using language fluently, and at other times a focus on grammar and accuracy is more relevant. Your choice will depend on many things, including your aims for the lesson, how your students like to learn and maybe even the time of day you are teaching! Perhaps your students need to move about a bit at the end of the day, so doing a role-play could be useful. For example, if your students have been learning the language of shopping then acting out a scene where they buy something would give them the opportunity to practise the language. Alternatively, a mingle activity to review some recent language might work well.

⊡ LESSON IDEA ONLINE 3.2: 'FIND SOMEONE WHO …'

This mingle activity using past tense question forms is active and involves students walking around the class to ask each other questions. This sort of activity can be used to practise lots of different language.

Accuracy or fluency?

We think about this when we plan the focus of our lessons. It might be a mix, or it might be both at different points in the lesson. It will influence the tasks and activities that we include in our lessons. While the two areas aren't totally separate, and it's possible to be very accurate and very fluent (and of course not accurate and not fluent!), most of the time we have an idea of which one we are focusing on in our lessons. To encourage fluency, for example in a lesson where you want to practise certain spoken language, you wouldn't interrupt students to correct them if you heard mistakes. This doesn't mean that you are ignoring errors. It's useful to make a note of any mistakes and then use them as feedback to the class, asking students to spot the errors and correct them, and as feedback for your own teaching.

Teacher Tip

You need to know what the focus of an activity is. Think about these examples from a coursebook and decide which one focuses on accuracy and which one focuses on fluency.

- You have just read about school rules in another country. Imagine you could make the rules for your school. Talk to your partner and discuss what they would be.
- Look at the following sentences about joining a sports club and the instructions for using the gym. Complete the sentences with your ideas.

Both of these activities would involve using modal verbs, particularly *must/mustn't/can/can't*. The first activity is freer and has a stronger focus on fluency. The second one is more controlled and so focuses more on accuracy.

Whatever approach we take, we need to keep in mind two areas of language ability or competence: **linguistic competence** and **communicative competence**. Linguistic competence is an understanding of why language is used as it is and the ability to recognise its function. Communicative competence is how students can communicate well and make themselves understood. Grammar and vocabulary are important but not useful if students can't use them to communicate! Our lessons need to balance the two areas.

Summary

Having considered the nature of teaching English, you now know that:

- Students are usually motivated by the use of English around them and recognise how they can use the language when they leave school.

- English may be used as the language of instruction for other subjects.

- We as teachers need to know about:

  - grammar, vocabulary and pronunciation

  - teaching the different skills

  - teaching for accuracy or fluency

  - our students.

Key considerations

4

Considerations for language teaching

In language we need to consider three key areas:

- Competence or ability – What does it mean to 'know' a language?
- Teaching approaches – How do we teach language?
- Grammar, vocabulary and pronunciation – What do we teach?

What does 'speaking English' mean?

First we need to think about the concept of what it means to 'speak a language'. It seems obvious, but do we all have the same ideas?

Teacher Tip

Take a minute to think about how you would describe what it means to 'speak a language'.

What is important for you as a teacher?

What is important to your students?

Are they the same things?

For example, your students may think the most important thing is to be able to speak to other people or to use social media in English. For you as a teacher, it may be more important that your students can use the grammar they have learnt when they participate in other lessons that are taught in English.

Your answer will probably depend on the students you teach. But most of us will want our students to *understand the language* and *have the confidence to use it*. Linguists split these two ideas and refer to linguistic competence *and* communicative competence (see Chapter 3 for more on this) and they are both important for our students. We need to think about how we balance these two areas. Sometimes, we will focus on one and at other times we will focus on the other. Ultimately, students need the right mix so that they can use English effectively. If this includes studying other subjects through English, then we need to make sure we teach in a way that allows them to do this.

How do we teach English?

People have been studying how languages are learnt for many years and are still looking for the full answer, but it is clear that learning a second language isn't like learning your first language. We don't spend months just listening to the language around us and then try out some simple sounds and words, like babies do. Young children don't have to learn what a past tense is, or learn which preposition to use with an adjective or how to pronounce a word. But these are exactly the things we teach our students.

There are a number of teaching approaches that view language learning differently. Here are some of the main ones.

The Grammar Translation Approach

The Grammar Translation Approach was defined in the mid–20th century and believes that translating language helps students to understand better. It saw language as a set of rules. Accuracy was the most important thing and it focused on reading and writing.

The Presentation, Practice and Production Approach (PPP)

The Presentation, Practice and Production Approach (PPP) takes a very structured view of how language should be taught. New language is presented to students in a context so that the meaning is clear. Then students practise it in a very controlled way. Finally, they are given a situation in which they practise it more freely. Accuracy is very important in this approach.

The Test-Teach-Test Approach (TTT)

The Test-Teach-Test Approach is useful for checking what your students already know. Here 'test' doesn't refer to a formal test. It means you give students something to do with the language to see how much they know, then highlight the language and retest by asking students to use it. Again, accuracy is most important in this approach.

The Lexical Approach

With the Lexical Approach vocabulary is more important than grammar and language is taught in chunks or phrases. Grammar is not ignored, though.

The Guided Discovery Approach

The idea behind the Guided Discovery Approach is that students learn best if they discover things for themselves. Teachers often present structures in a text and ask students to work out rules from what they read or listen to.

The Communicative Approach

The Communicative Approach states that communication is the most important thing. Often functions are key to communicative lessons, e.g. asking for things in shops, apologising to someone. Fluency is very important in this approach.

Teacher Tip

Think about the last lesson you taught and consider whether it included just one of these approaches or parts of more than one.

Can you find activities where students had to communicate with each other?

Was there a task focusing on vocabulary?

Were there any activities where students had to work out grammar rules from text they were given?

Was there a task that gave controlled practice of language after it had been presented?

In fact, nowadays most of us probably use all of these approaches in different ways at different times. It's important for us to consider these approaches as they influence the way we teach and plan our lessons. There are probably good things from each approach that you use in your teaching.

Let's have a look at an example of an activity related to one approach, using Lesson idea online 4.1.

☑ LESSON IDEA ONLINE 4.1: LEXICAL CHUNKS: *GET*

This activity focuses on **lexical chunks,** which are an important part of the Lexical Approach. These are phrases that we teach as one whole to make sure students remember the whole phrase. This lesson uses a short reading task to demonstrate the language.

Making errors

Some of the approaches assume it's more important to be accurate than to be fluent. Nowadays in language learning most of us realise that error is in fact very important. Making mistakes or errors in a language is an important part of language learning. It shows that students are trying new language and are being adventurous. The types of error students make also provide useful feedback and help inform how we plan future learning.

Teacher Tip

Think about some of the errors you have heard your students make in class.

Why do you think they made them?

It might be that they have thought about what that language is like in their first language and have translated. It could be that they have learnt a rule for some language and have applied it to other language, for example: using the *–ed* past tense ending for all verbs – *He eated*. Or maybe they have been trying out language to see if it is correct.

How do you manage errors?

There isn't just one way to manage errors. It will depend on the aims of your lesson and whether you are focusing on fluency rather than accuracy in that particular part of your lesson. Even if you hear language that you think students should be getting right, but aren't, you need to think about *when* and *how* to correct it. In Chapter 7 we will look at how sometimes it is better to make a note of errors for future use.

I sometimes find that lots of students have been making a similar error and realise that for some reason something hasn't been understood. In that situation it's no good just correcting on the spot. We have to think about how to re-teach the point.

What to teach?

We can break down the areas that we teach into the following:

1 grammar
2 vocabulary (also known as lexis)
3 pronunciation
4 coherence.

We don't usually teach the different areas completely separately from each other, but it is useful sometimes to think of them separately.

1. Grammar

Every language teacher knows they have to have a good understanding of grammar, and there are three things to think about for any structure:

* form
* function
* phonology.

Teacher Tip

Let's look at an example of what that means and how we can break it down for our students.

How to analyse grammar – the modal verb *can*

e.g. *She can swim well.*

- Form: *Can* is a modal verb and is an auxiliary, but it doesn't change for third person singular use like other auxiliary verbs.
- Function: Here it shows ability but of course *can* is also used for other functions, like requests.
- Phonology: The vowel sound for the 'a' in *can* changes with the positive and negative. In fact, it has three different pronunciations:

She can swim. /ʃɪː kən swɪm/

She can't swim.   /ʃɪː kɑːnt swɪm/

Can she swim?   /kən ʃɪː swɪm/   *Yes she can.* /jes ʃɪ kæn/

The article *Integrating pronunciation into classroom activities* on the British Council website gives lots of different ideas for integrating pronunciation into our teaching.

Already, we can see that what looks like an easy grammatical structure has a lot for students to learn about.

Aspect

One of the most useful concepts of language that we can teach our students is the idea of aspect in English.

If we think of tenses telling us *when* something happened, then aspect shows a *perspective* on the action. The two aspects we use are the *continuous* aspect and the *perfect* aspect. You can read more about these two aspects on the English grammar section of the British Council website.

A continuous aspect generally means that a longer action is interrupted by another event or a point in time. A perfect aspect generally means that something happened before another event or point in time. See Figure 4.1 and Figure 4.2 for how timelines demonstrate the concepts of continuous and perfect aspect.

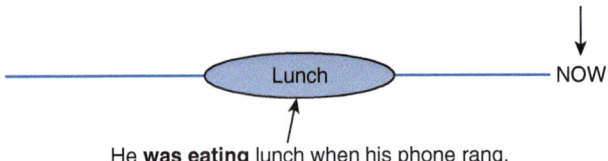

He **was eating** lunch when his phone rang.

Figure 4.1: Continuous aspect

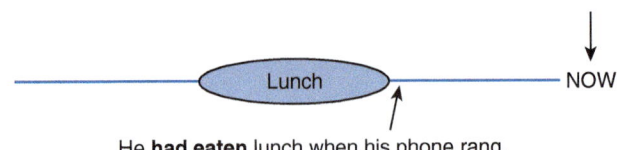

He **had eaten** lunch when his phone rang.

Figure 4.2: Perfect aspect

This way of showing the concept of the continuous and perfect aspects often makes it very clear to students very quickly. It's particularly helpful for students who have a strong visual sense.

Here the examples are in the past tense, but the same concept applies for all time references, present, past or future. If we can make concepts like this clear to our students when they learn the present tenses, then this will help them when they come to look at aspect in the past and future, too.

Teacher Tip

Think about the last time you taught a continuous or perfect tense to your students and the examples you gave to show them the language. Draw timelines for these examples.

Look at Lesson idea online 6.5 on present perfect tenses to see how timelines can be used in classroom activities.

It's interesting when other languages have similar grammatical structures to ours. We may think this makes English easier. This might be true, but often, even if something similar exists, it is used differently. We need to make sure we recognise this when it occurs. It is sometimes easier to learn something totally new than to think about how something is used differently.

2. Vocabulary

We can use the same approach of thinking about form, function and phonology when we teach vocabulary.

Teacher Tip

How to analyse vocabulary – *information*

e.g. *Where can I find information on this city?*

- Form: This is the spelling of the word as well as prefixes or suffixes that help to form the word.
- Function: It's an uncountable noun that can be made into a countable phrase, as in *two pieces of information.*
  It's also useful to point out that it's often shortened to *info* in everyday, less formal English.
- Phonology: The phonology of the word including the pronunciation and the word stress:
  information /ˌɪnfəˈmeɪʃən/ – four syllables with the primary stress on the third syllable giving the stress pattern ooOo.

You can find some useful material to help you teach this area by searching for 'stress and intonation' on the internet.

We all know there is more to think about than these three areas when we think about a word. We need to teach students what other words it is often seen with, for example *information desk*, or *further information*. This is referred to as **collocation**. Think back to the earlier part of this chapter, when we talked about the Lexical Approach, and you'll recognise that collocation is seen as very important there.

Information is quite a neutral word so it doesn't have a particular connotation, but if you think of these three synonyms: *slim, thin, skinny*, you'll see that they each have a slightly different meaning associated with them. While *thin* is fairly neutral, *slim* is positive and *skinny* is negative. This is an area that we need to teach our students about so they don't offend anyone!

When they learn a new word students will also need to know whether it has a homophone (for example: *A cat has four **paws**. / Let's **pause** for a moment.*) or a homonym (*In Japan people **bow** when they meet. / He tied the ribbon in a **bow**.*) It's also useful for students to learn if the word is a false friend. For example, the word for 'bookshop' in French, *librairie*, is very similar to the word *library* in English. The meanings are similar here but certainly not the same.

> **☑ LESSON IDEA ONLINE 4.2: WORD BUILDING**
>
> This is a good way of helping students to record everything they need to about a new word and it helps them to be active learners, too. It can be used at all levels and helps to encourage them to be independent in their learning.

3. Pronunciation

Now we need to think about pronunciation. We all know English pronunciation isn't regular (and isn't easy!). The **International Phonetic Alphabet (IPA)** is a useful tool to help us teach pronunciation. It sets out all of the different sounds of English and is a useful resource for students.

> **☑ LESSON IDEA ONLINE 4.3: SOUNDS: INTRODUCING THE IPA**
>
> This lesson idea shows how you could introduce the idea of the IPA and the individual sounds to your students. They are actively involved in producing their own IPA chart, which they will complete over a series of lessons as new sounds are introduced. This activity uses the Guided Discovery Approach mentioned earlier.

Once your students understand the IPA you can incorporate elements of it into different lessons, which will help them with their pronunciation of individual sounds.

> **☑ LESSON IDEA ONLINE 4.4: SOUNDS: MINIMAL PAIRS**
>
> This activity focuses on minimal pairs – two words that only have one sound different in them and so can sometimes be confused in speaking.

Possibly more important in the area of pronunciation are *sentence stress* and *intonation*. Research has shown that native speakers of English are very tolerant of mistakes in grammar, vocabulary and spelling when they see them. However, they are less aware of how sentence stress and intonation are used and so misunderstandings can happen. Sometimes non-native speakers can seem abrupt or even rude just because they are using different intonation patterns.

Teacher Tip

Listen to some recordings from your coursebook or online. Think about where the stress is placed in words and the sentences, how fast the speaker is talking and what intonation they are using. Could you use this to focus on the mood and emotions of the speakers to help students understand intonation more? You could give students a simple phrase to say with different emotions to help them develop a greater awareness of how important intonation is. For example:

Phrase: *It's Monday.*

Emotions: surprise, excitement, disappointment, confusion.

---

4. Coherence

In Chapter 3 we looked at how we can't presume that students automatically carry the skills they have in their first language over to a second language. We looked at highlighting skills in reading to help them with this. Similarly, we also need to guide students with *coherence*. Coherence refers to how a text, spoken or written, flows and sounds like a whole text rather than a series of sentences. It is often an area that teachers forget about, but I think it's one of the most valuable things for students. It's particularly useful for more advanced students but is relevant to all levels.

Teacher Tip

Read Texts A and B.

A. I got up late this morning and I had to rush to get to school on time. The bus I get to take me to school didn't come on time either. The bus was busy, too. I got on the bus and asked the bus driver for a ticket. The bus driver said he didn't have any change. I didn't have any change. The bus driver told me I had to get off the bus. I had to walk to school. I was very late.

B. I got up late this morning and had to rush to get to school on time. The bus I get to take me there didn't come on time either. It was busy, too. I got on and asked the bus driver for a ticket. He said he didn't have any change. I didn't have any coins and he told me I had to get off. I had to walk to school so I was very late.

Which one sounds more natural?

The first thing we notice is that Text B has fewer words than Text A. It has the same content, though. Writing coherently often means writing more concisely, too. Text B is also easier to read. It uses pronouns instead of repeating nouns, for example: *the bus driver – he*. It also uses substitution, for example: *change – coins*. This avoids repetition. There are also conjunctions linking ideas in the text, for example: '... *so I was ....*'

So, the features that help us to highlight coherent texts are:

- referencing – use of pronouns
- substitution – using synonyms to avoid repeating a word or idea
- sequencing – words/phrases that show the order of events, e.g. *firstly, afterwards*
- contrasting – words/phrases to show two ideas are linked but have different viewpoints or ideas, e.g. *but, although*
- explanations – words/phrases that show two sentences are linked with a reason, e.g. *thus, so*
- examples – words/phrases that indicate an idea is going to be supported, e.g. *for example, one example is*
- result – words/phrases that indicate an outcome is going to follow, e.g. *therefore, hence.*

I have a word of caution to add here. When we teach students these words, sometimes they overuse them. One example that comes to mind is *moreover*. I always tell students that I very rarely use this word and do so only in more formal writing, but they seem to like it and I frequently find it in written work. I think this is because the idea of coherence isn't often taught at lower levels, so when students find these words, they think this is the key to coherence and either overuse or misuse them. We can put this right by including work on coherence from early stages.

▣ LESSON IDEA ONLINE 4.5: COHESION IN WRITING

In this lesson idea we look at cohesion of written language.

This activity is for upper intermediate students but can be adapted for any level by changing the text.

Summary

Having considered the *key considerations* of language teaching, you now know:

- What we want our students to focus on – being accurate *or* fluent.

- The methodology we use for teaching and the rationale behind it.

- Some concepts relating to the language that we teach and how to help students use these successfully.

5 | Interpreting a syllabus

What is a syllabus?

Before we start to think about how to interpret a syllabus we should clarify what we mean by the term 'syllabus'. At the most basic level it is what we teach over a period of time, usually an academic year. This may be determined by a national or locally agreed curriculum, or your school may have more flexibility in deciding what is on the curriculum. In this chapter we are going to look at what is contained in the syllabus published by exam boards and awarding bodies and how these can support your teaching. The syllabus documents are usually available online and give vital information to allow you to plan your teaching programme for the year (see Figure 5.1).

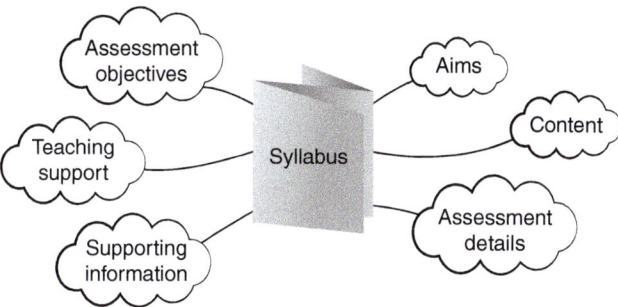

Figure 5.1

- **The overall aims of the syllabus** – These are stated at a high level such as '*to develop learners' ability to use English effectively for the purpose of practical communication*'. The aims won't tell you how to teach but you should check that these aims are consistent with what you are teaching.
- **The content** – A good syllabus will have a positive impact on your classroom practice so will include a focus on all four language skills: reading, writing, listening and speaking. The syllabus should also give a breakdown of what is expected for each of these skills. For example, for writing you may find '*select and organise relevant information and ideas into paragraphs and use appropriate linking devices*'. This information will help you to focus your teaching to fit the syllabus and the end assessment.
- **The details of the assessment** – This will include information about the number of components there are, the task types that they

will have, how many marks each task will have and details of what students are expected to do in the test itself.

- **The assessment objectives** – A valid assessment tests what it says it will test. Therefore the assessment objectives will show how the content is to be assessed. We would expect the example of content for writing mentioned above to be part of an assessment objective for writing.

- **Teaching support** – Example questions and mark schemes can often be found in the syllabus documents or you may find links to where you can get these. There may also be details of where you can access teaching guidance to help you prepare your students for the assessment, as well as details of any professional development opportunities.

- **Supporting information** – Other useful information that should be shown includes the expected level of the students at the start of the course and at the end, an estimate of how many teaching hours it may take to reach the expected end level and practical details about dates for exams.

Planning your teaching

Planning is a key skill for us as teachers. We need to be able to see the whole syllabus and imagine how this can be broken down into smaller parts for our daily teaching. At the highest level, we think about how the overall course will work. At the other end of the spectrum we plan how an individual activity will work (see Figure 5.2).

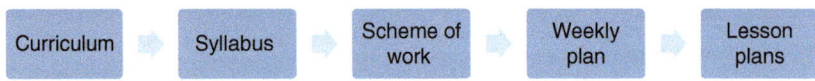

Figure 5.2

I use a scheme of work as an overall plan for the course I am teaching. I construct it at the start of the course. It is time-consuming to do but gives me the confidence to know how I will cover all of the language that I need to and include a good balance of skills and topics. I use set headings on my scheme of work to make sure I think of everything, as shown in Table 5.1.

Week	Context/ topic	Teaching aims	Links to AOs	Language	Skills	Resources	Assessment opportunities

Table 5.1

Be prepared to change your scheme of work. Having a plan doesn't mean that you should stick to it rigidly. You may find your class needs more or less time on something. Maybe something topical happens that you want to include or you respond to the interests of your class and change the focus of a lesson.

From the scheme of work you can then look at how the content for a month or week can be broken down into individual lessons and you can produce your lesson plans from this. The headings given to the lesson ideas in this book will guide you in your planning at this level.

We have a lot to think about when we plan our lessons (see Figure 5.3). Using the scheme of work along with exam syllabus information, and particularly the assessment objectives (AOs), will make sure that we are preparing our students well for their final assessment as well as making sure that the topics and contexts we use are interesting.

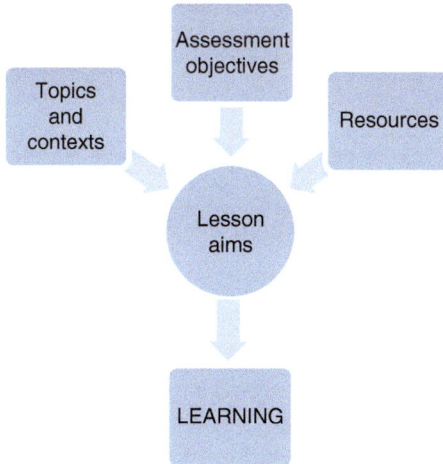

Figure 5.3

Pace is a key consideration. If you don't cover enough in the first part of the year, your teaching will be rushed later on. As you get to know your students you will be able to make a judgement on this and may choose to adjust your scheme of work accordingly. This could mean that you don't have enough time to cover everything that you planned to. But you need to be careful not to rush too much to fit a schedule either. If you do, you may not give your students enough time to learn well. When I teach a course I find I am continually returning to my plans to make adjustments based on what is actually happening in class. If you take the approach of **Plan–Do–Review** this will help. You can apply this at lesson level and think about how a lesson has gone and what amendments you may need to make to later teaching. You should also review at regular points in the course to see if your overall syllabus plan for the year needs amending. Having these review stages in mind helps you to reflect on your aims and your teaching.

A good course that interests students and also motivates them to learn will have variety. When you plan at a weekly, monthly or termly level you can look across your plans and make sure you have enough variety to keep everyone interested. At the same time, some routine is also useful to give students confidence and security in their learning. As with many of the things we have discussed, it is a matter of getting the right balance.

When we consider all of these elements we can make sure our lesson aims focus on what our students need to be successful. Of course this doesn't just mean teaching 'for the assessment'. A good assessment that has been chosen to fit the needs of your students, and that matches how they will use English, is a strong supporting tool for your teaching.

Choosing your material

While some of us are able to choose the coursebook we teach from, others may have it chosen for them. Luckily there are many excellent coursebooks published these days that provide really interesting lessons for us to use. Most of them are aimed at particular age groups, which helps to make sure that the material is relevant. However, I have never found a book that exactly matched what I wanted to teach to a class for the whole year. You need to check that material is suitable for the age group you are teaching, is culturally relevant and is interesting for your class. Often you can find an alternative way of covering some language or skills from other books. When I look at a unit of a coursebook, I think about how the content will help my students achieve their goals and work towards the learning and assessment objectives. If there are activities that I think won't meet those needs, or if I think the subject or task won't be suitable, I may decide not to use them. Or I may decide to adapt the activity in some way to make it work. Introducing material that is personalised is a great way to provide really relevant content for your lessons. It is very time-consuming to write your own material, though, so I always make sure that it is something that I can use again and again to get maximum value from it. Of course you can involve your students in writing material for classroom use, which is very valuable.

Coursebooks are usually clearly signposted to show what the focus is of a lesson or parts of a lesson.

Teacher Tip

Look at your coursebook and check that you can identify the different parts of a unit.

- Is the grammar focus clear?
- Is there a section on vocabulary?
- What skills are practised?
- Does the unit have any functional language included?
- Does all of the content fit with your overall syllabus?

However you decide to interpret your syllabus, and however much control you have over the design, one thing to keep in mind is the need to be flexible. Nothing that involves working with people ever goes exactly to plan all of the time.

Teacher Tip

Think about these situations and how they impact on your teaching.

- Your students are really tired at the end of a week and can't focus on the lesson well.
- You have been off sick for a week and your class has been covered by different teachers each day.

- You realise that the material you used to teach a new language point didn't work as well as you had hoped. You need to re-teach this language.
- Your students were really enthusiastic about an activity and it went on for much longer than you had planned.
- There was a fire alarm and you lost a whole lesson.

If any of these have happened to you, it will have had an impact on your plans for the lesson, the week or maybe even the year. We always need to build in some contingency time when we plan a syllabus to allow for this. Having to rush through the last weeks of a course means these areas won't be taught well.

Revisiting language

A feature of any syllabus, however we design it, is to remember that teaching something once doesn't mean our students will have learnt everything about it, or that they will remember it and will use it straight away. As teachers, it can seem frustrating to think about revisiting language and skills to reinforce them, but it is vital. Educationalists now refer to a **spiral curriculum**, shown in Figure 5.4, to recognise this.

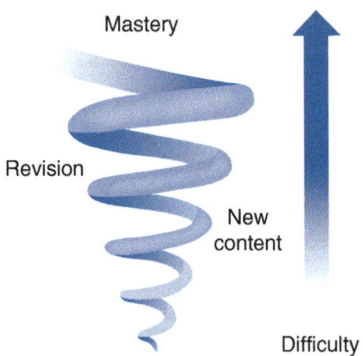

Figure 5.4

When we revisit language, we might add new contexts or uses as our expectations get higher and our students remember more each time. Whatever the subject, nothing is mastered in one go! Many coursebooks now include this approach and you will see language being recycled to support the spiral curriculum.

Summary

Thinking about interpreting a syllabus and planning how to implement it, you now know:

- what syllabuses are and why we need them

- what we can find in syllabus documents

- how to use this information to help plan our teaching

- how to view our coursebooks

- why we need contingency time in the syllabus.

6

Active learning

What is active learning?

Active learning is a pedagogical practice that places student learning at its centre. It focuses on *how* students learn, not just on *what* they learn. We as teachers need to encourage students to 'think hard', rather than passively receive information. Active learning encourages students to take responsibility for their learning and supports them in becoming independent and confident learners in school and beyond.

Research shows us that it is not possible to transmit understanding to students by simply telling them what they need to know. Instead, we need to make sure that we challenge students' thinking and support them in building their own understanding. Active learning encourages more complex thought processes, such as evaluating, analysing and synthesising, which foster a greater number of neural connections in the brain. While some students may be able to create their own meaning from information received passively, others will not. Active learning enables all students to build knowledge and understanding in response to the opportunities we provide.

Why adopt an active learning approach?

We can enrich all areas of the curriculum, at all stages, by embedding an active learning approach.

In active learning, we need to think not only about the content but also about the process. It gives students greater involvement and control over their learning. This encourages all students to stay focused on their learning, which will often give them greater enthusiasm for their studies. Active learning is intellectually stimulating and taking this approach encourages a level of academic discussion with our students that we, as teachers, can also enjoy. Healthy discussion means that students are engaging with us as a partner in their learning.

Students will better be able to revise for examinations in the sense that revision really is 're-vision' of the ideas that they already understand.

Active learning develops students' analytical skills, supporting them to be better problem solvers and more effective in their application of knowledge. They will be prepared to deal with challenging and unexpected situations. As a result, students are more confident in continuing to learn once they have left school and are better equipped for the transition to higher education and the workplace.

What are the challenges of incorporating active learning?

When people start thinking about putting active learning into practice, they often make the mistake of thinking more about the activity they want to design than about the learning. The most important thing is to put the student and the learning at the centre of our planning. A task can be quite simple but still get the student to think critically and independently. Sometimes a complicated task does not actually help to develop the students' thinking or understanding at all. We need to consider carefully what we want our students to learn or understand and then shape the task to activate this learning.

What makes a 'successful' language learner?

Before we start to think about what active learning looks like in the language classroom, let's imagine the 'successful' language learner. What would we expect them to be able to do and to be confident about? This will help us to focus on how we can help them to achieve this.

Teacher Tip

Look at the following list. Think about which of these statements describe a successful language learner.

1 Wants to understand every word that they read.
2 Takes every opportunity to communicate in English, even if it is difficult.
3 Never makes any mistakes.
4 Asks for clarification if they don't understand something.
5 Only uses language they are sure is correct.
6 Tries out new language, even if they are unsure of it.

We will all take different priorities from this list and your decisions will depend on the situation you teach in. However, in principle points 1, 3 and 5 reflect a more traditional approach to language learning, while the other points, 2, 4 and 6, are now felt to be features of a successful, communicative language learner.

We need to remember that a successful language learner is not necessarily the student who is most accurate and makes no mistakes in using the language. Successful language learners can communicate – whatever their level of language ability. Using tasks that follow the principles of active learning will help them to practise communication skills in the classroom, but that doesn't mean that active learning isn't useful for learning grammar and vocabulary, too. We can teach these areas with tasks that are student-centred and that are designed to make sure our class is active. This will make the learning more enjoyable as well as more effective.

Different ways students learn

Next we need to think about how we can help students to achieve this expertise in communication. The first thing to think about is that there are many different ways of learning and no one of them is better than the others. We don't all learn in the same way. What works for one student may not work for another and, just as importantly, what works for *you* might not work for your students. Our active learning tasks will clearly need to incorporate many different ways of learning to make sure everyone in the class can benefit.

Teacher Tip

Think about a class you teach now and think about any students who show a particular way of learning language. Maybe they write things down straight away, or maybe they repeat things to themselves.

Make sure you allow for this in your lessons by using lots of different ways to engage them. This could include:

- using pictures, flashcards and well set out working on the board
- giving time for students to repeat new vocabulary
- providing opportunities for students to get up and move around while using language.

Of course, you can't use all of these in every lesson, but by keeping a balance you can consider all the students in your class.

In addition, there will be students who like to have time to reflect on what they are learning and who like to be given choices in how they approach a task, while others prefer to be spontaneous and respond immediately. Some students have a preference for working in groups, while others prefer working alone. However, students may not fall into the same group all of the time and may change their preference depending on how they feel, what they are studying or the task they are doing. So, our teaching needs to be varied and we need to think about all of these styles to keep every student motivated and engaged.

Students need different strategies or ways to learn. You can help them to be aware of these and to choose the ones that work best for them. There is no best technique for learning language. The examples of active learning activities that are included in this chapter demonstrate a range of different learning strategies that are relevant to different learning preferences.

What do we need to make sure that active language learning takes place?

Of course we need to have the skills to present tasks so that students can be active. The examples in this chapter and the accompanying lesson ideas will help to highlight these, but something that is just as important is to think about how your students will respond to these tasks. I have found that students who are used to waiting for language to be presented to them can sometimes be reluctant at first. However, they soon see that this different way of taking part in lessons is actually more interesting and more fun. It helps if you explain to students why they are doing something in this way, for example explaining how much more language practice they get when they compare answers with a partner after doing a reading comprehension exercise, rather than waiting for you to tell them what is right or wrong.

I've met teachers who feel that the limitations of their classroom make active learning difficult. I think we'd all like to be teaching in huge classrooms with lots of resources, but in fact this isn't always needed for effective active language learning to take place. More often it's about how we see the task we want students to do, rather than having students moving around physically.

Some teachers feel that active learning takes up too much valuable time. They worry that they have so much to teach on the syllabus that it is going to be impossible to use active tasks, but there is plenty of research and evidence to show that students who take an active role in their learning understand language more quickly and remember things better. So, if we spend less time reviewing and possibly re-teaching structures, vocabulary and approaches to skills, this is a good time investment for us all.

Language teaching has followed a communicative approach (see Chapter 4 **Key considerations**) since the 1970s and this has active learning at its core. It is likely that you are using active learning in your classroom now, even if you aren't aware of it. The rest of this chapter looks at some typical tasks and activities and highlights the features of active learning that they use.

How do we recognise active learning?

Our classrooms can be active in many different ways. Students might be active because they are finding information from a particular source, for example a reading text, when they are talking to each other in pair work, or are being active in individual work to plan their own learning, working in silence. It is all positive as long as their *brains* are focused on language and are active.

This doesn't mean that you as the teacher are doing any less, however! It might mean that there is less focus on *you* in the classroom itself. This is positive and will allow you to assess how your students are doing, who has learnt something well and which students need more time to be able to use language more suitably. Tasks that promote active learning sometimes take a little longer to produce and plan, but they can be used again and again, probably with some modification so, in the long term, this is a good time investment. As with any task you use, the most important thing is *what* you are trying to help your students to learn. If this is lost while you focus on making sure your students are active, then nothing has been gained. It is important to keep checking your lesson aims and the learning objectives for your lesson.

Language skills

Let's start by thinking about the four language skills: the receptive skills of reading and listening and the productive skills of writing and speaking. It is hard to imagine our students being passive while doing tasks related to these skills, but we can still make sure we get maximum benefit from them by planning carefully.

In some activities we as teachers become fairly passive as students run the activity themselves. The teacher's role is to monitor and note down things that we hear for future reference (we'll talk about this more in Chapter 7 **Assessment for Learning**).

> ☑ **LESSON IDEA ONLINE 6.1: PYRAMID DISCUSSION: CAMPING**
>
> In this activity the focus is on fluency. A situation is provided with a task and students need to talk together to complete the activity. This can be adapted to any level with a different situation. It is a good activity for giving students the opportunity to use language of persuasion and of justifying their choices.

Jigsaw activities are popular in coursebooks and are often used in language classrooms. In these activities students only have part of the information they need to complete the whole task. Like a jigsaw, it is only when the pieces are put together that you see the whole picture. This means that students need to talk to each other to complete the task so speaking skills are practised too. With jigsaw reading, students read texts with different information, and in jigsaw listening, they listen to different information.

Teacher Tip

Look in the coursebook you are using and see if it has a jigsaw reading task. You often find they are labelled as Student A and Student B activities and are added at the back of the book to stop students spoiling the activity by reading both texts!

If there isn't a jigsaw reading task, you could create one by making two versions of a text and asking students to read and then discuss the differences. There are plenty of jigsaw tasks to download and use for free on websites such as ESL Jigsaws.

At higher levels, the two reading texts could be articles from different newspapers about the same topic but with a different point of view. Or you could ask students to find an article on a topic themselves and to bring it to class to use. This will involve them even more in the learning process, but you will need to make sure that they don't all do the same internet search and choose the same article!

☑ LESSON IDEA ONLINE 6.2: JIGSAW READING

This is a jigsaw reading task for lower level students. The focus is on the past tense and there is a task to complete which the students can only do if they share the content of their text. This creates an **information gap** as students can't answer the questions at the end of the text on their own. The students need to work together to complete the questions and, with an element of problem solving, this is a very student-centred activity. Students are very active during this activity and use all four skills, as well as focusing on the past tense and vocabulary related to shopping.

This activity is quite controlled and you should know exactly what to expect your students to do and what the outcome will be. This is quite different from the speaking task in Lesson idea online 6.1.

Grammar

It is easy to see how tasks and activities that relate to the four language skills involve the principles of active learning. But how do we use these principles in teaching grammar? An example of active learning with grammar is how we can use what students already know to present new grammar. This **scaffolding** allows students to build on their existing knowledge and understanding.

Teacher Tip

As an example, the simple present tense is usually one of the first structures to be taught at a low level. But we don't teach all of its uses at once.

Look at these four uses of the simple present tense and think about what level you would teach them at.

1 He lives in a big house.
2 He often goes to play football on Fridays.
3 The film starts in ten minutes.
4 So, he walks into the shop, and asks for the manager.

The first example describes a present state. The second refers to a repeated activity, in the past and future, but doesn't refer to what is happening at this exact moment. The third example talks about the future, and in the last example we are describing something in the past. As many people say, the simple present isn't really that simple and isn't usually present! The first two examples are usually found in courses for beginners or elementary students. The use of the simple present for the future is often taught at pre-intermediate or intermediate level. The final example shows an advanced use of the tense being used to tell a story. However, the form is the same for all of these uses and so when we introduce a new use students are able to build on what they already know. This is known as **scaffolding** and is a useful concept for us to remember when we plan active learning tasks.

Guided discovery

The use of a Guided Discovery Approach is useful in these cases (see Chapter 4 **Key considerations** for more details) but as you will see in the following example we can help students to work out how language is used. Here, the difference between *will* and *going to* for future use is shown. This can be a difficult distinction for students to make, but with carefully written examples the meaning should be clear.

Teacher Tip

Guided discovery of meaning – *will* and *going to*

The following dialogue could be given to students to discuss with a partner or in groups to see if they can work out the difference in meaning.

Jack: *Oh no! We don't have any coffee left.*

Maria: *Oh really? Well, **I'll buy** some at the supermarket this afternoon.*

Jack: *That's great. I wonder if Luca needs anything at the supermarket. I'll phone him and ask.*

Jack: *Luca, do you need any shopping?*

Luca: *Yes! There's no coffee in the cupboard.*

Jack: *It's okay. Maria **is going to buy** some this afternoon.*

By providing a context (shopping) and a time frame (present and future) you are *guiding* students in their discussion. Giving students two sentences on their own, for example *I'll buy some coffee this afternoon/I'm going to buy some coffee this afternoon*, would be much more difficult. With the short dialogue, students are able to use their problem-solving skills to try to work out that *will* is used when making a decision and *going to* is used when the decision has already been made, however recently, and is a plan. Of course, in doing this, your students are practising their spoken English as well as thinking about grammar.

Concept questions can be used to draw out the meaning and to make sure it is clear to everyone in the class. Usually, we try to avoid asking closed questions when we promote active learning, but concept questions have a different function. They are used to check understanding and we'll look at them more in Chapter 7 **Assessment for Learning**. Two simple concept questions for the example we have used above are:

When did Maria find out there was no coffee?

When did she make the decision to buy some?

This approach for presenting new language is effective as students invest time in analysing the language and are engaged and active. Research shows that in these conditions students remember much more than if they are simply given language, examples and explanation. It's much easier for us to see if they have understood it as well.

☑ LESSON IDEA ONLINE 6.3: GRAMMAR PRACTICE: *WILL/GOING TO*

This is an activity you could use to practise the distinction between *will* and *going to* once you feel your students have understood the language. It personalises the language, which makes it more interesting for students. You could use it after you have taught the structures in a lesson, to check how well students have remembered them in a later lesson or as a revision activity.

Peer-teaching vocabulary

We can use active learning tasks to check understanding and to revise language. I often ask students to explain the use of grammar or the meaning of vocabulary to each other. This encourages them to take responsibility for and ownership of their learning. Here are two lesson ideas that use this principle. One of them focuses on grammar and the other on vocabulary.

☑ LESSON IDEA ONLINE 6.4: PEER-TEACHING VOCABULARY

In this student-centred activity students research the meaning of words or phrases and then teach them to other students. This activity can take as little as 25 minutes but could be extended to suit the ability of your students and the lesson time available.

> ☑ **LESSON IDEA ONLINE 6.5: GRAMMAR: PRESENT PERFECT TENSES**
>
> This activity is very student-centred and is a good example of how to actively revise language in class.

An active classroom is a successful classroom for our students and for us, too. Students learn more and, importantly, remember better because they have played an active role in how they learn. That's satisfying for everyone. It is also better for us as teachers. You should find that you do less talking in the classroom as the students do more. Active learning means we need to make sure we plan well in advance of the lesson and remain active in monitoring what our students are doing during the activities.

Summary

Now that we've looked at active learning, you will have a good understanding of:

- How being active helps our students to be successful language learners.

- What active learning looks like in practice.

- How we can make our classrooms more student-centred.

Assessment for Learning

7

What is Assessment for Learning?

Assessment for Learning (AfL) is a teaching approach that generates feedback that can be used to improve students' performance. Students become more involved in the learning process and, from this, gain confidence in what they are expected to learn and to what standard. We as teachers gain insights into a student's level of understanding of a particular concept or topic, which helps to inform how we support their progression.

We need to understand the meaning and method of giving purposeful feedback to optimise learning. Feedback can be informal, such as oral comments to help students think through problems, or formal, such as the use of rubrics to help clarify and scaffold learning and assessment objectives.

Why use Assessment for Learning?

By following well-designed approaches to AfL, we can understand better how our students are learning and use this to plan what we will do next with a class or individual students (see Figure 7.1). We can help our students to see what they are aiming for and to understand what they need to do to get there. AfL makes learning visible; it helps students understand more accurately the nature of the material they are learning and themselves as learners. The quality of interactions and feedback between students and teachers becomes critical to the learning process.

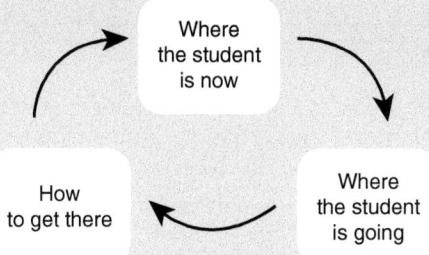

Figure 7.1: How can we use this plan to help our students?

We can use AfL to help our students focus on specific elements of their learning and to take greater responsibility for how they might move forward. AfL creates a valuable connection between assessment and learning activities, as the clarification of objectives will have a direct impact on how we devise teaching and learning strategies. AfL techniques can support students in becoming more confident in what they are learning, reflective in how they are learning, more likely to try out new approaches, and more engaged in what they are being asked to learn.

What are the challenges of incorporating AfL?

The use of AfL does not mean that we need to test students more frequently. It would be easy to just increase the amount of summative assessment and use this formatively as a regular method of helping us decide what to do next in our teaching. We can judge how much learning has taken place through ways other than testing, including, above all, communicating with our students in a variety of ways and getting to know them better as individuals.

Assessing understanding

It's actually hard to think of a time when we *don't* assess learning in our classrooms. When we check that our students have understood instructions for a task, or when we listen to them doing a task or activity, we are making an assessment to see if they understand. It's a part of our teaching every day.

Non-teachers might suggest that we just ask the students if they understand. This might sound straightforward enough, but as teachers we know that we don't always get a true picture from simply asking whether students understand, as some students might not want to admit that they don't understand, while others may think they understand but in fact don't. We can't really tell from their answers. That doesn't mean that questioning isn't a valuable thing to do. We just need to think about how we do it and the types of question we use. And once we've done that we need to use the information formatively to think about where our lesson moves. It could be that everyone in the class has shown that they understand and you may need to make the later parts of your lesson more challenging. Or it could mean that you need to think about how to reinforce a point or even return to it later. This is what changes assessment *of* learning into assessment *for* learning. It isn't the task or the question we ask: it's what we do with the information we get.

Teacher Tip

Think of a time when you presented some new language, vocabulary or grammar.

- How did you check that your students understood what you wanted them to understand?
  - Think about whether you were checking understanding of the form of the language, the sounds involved and how the language is used.
  - Think about how you can be sure that everyone in the class understood. Did you listen to all students? Did you ask someone to give you an example so that everyone in the class could hear? What other ways did you use to check that everyone understood?

- What action did you take if they didn't all understand?
  - Think about whether you decided to review the language later in that lesson, or to check understanding again after students had time to think more, or whether you tried to give more examples.

Using questions in the classroom

When we ask a question, we want an answer, and in open questions it's tempting to take the first answer that the class offers. Maybe this comes from the strongest student, or the quickest student, or perhaps just from the students who have been paying attention! We might presume that students who haven't raised their hand don't know the answer. But is this true? Research shows that leaving a 'wait time' after asking a question of at least three seconds gives thinking time. This allows more students to realise that they do know the answer and to contribute. And you may find you get better, more considered answers from stronger students, too. It might feel like a long time to wait when you have silence in the classroom, but it's a very valuable silence. Once your students get used to this thinking time, it quickly becomes normal and doesn't feel strange.

Even if we get a correct answer, does everyone understand? Maybe, but maybe not. You need to observe your class carefully to see whether there are students who haven't understood but don't have the confidence to say so. It can mean you need to find another opportunity to check understanding. And, of course, if you get the right answer to a question, it might have just been a guess by the student, so we should always reinforce their answer by making it clear why the answer is correct. You might do this yourself, or maybe ask students to explain why to each other, or get another student to explain to the whole class.

Questioning is a valuable tool if we use it well. An example is the use of concept questions when teaching language. These are the type of closed yes/no question that we might usually avoid. However, they give students a clear understanding of the key features of a piece of language, whether it is structure or vocabulary.

Teacher Tip

Imagine you are teaching the present continuous to a group of beginners and have used this example:

She is riding a bicycle.

The following concept questions can help to check understanding:

Is it happening now?	Yes
Has she finished?	No
Does she do it every day?	Don't know
Is it in the past, present or future?	Present

This establishes the use of the present continuous and shows students that it is different from the present simple, for example.

In these examples we are checking learning *immediately*. Sometimes we won't want to assess learning as soon as this. We may check it later in the lesson or in another lesson. This helps us to find out how much has been understood and remembered. I often find it useful to check learning a few lessons later. Our students have a lot of new information given to them every day when considering the number of subjects they study. We can't presume that because we have taught something once, they will all automatically remember it and be able to use it. In fact, there is evidence now that says students need to use, see or hear new language many times before it really becomes a 'known' part of their active language. Different research suggests different numbers of times – and of course the context in which the students are studying will have an impact on this – but it is at least 15 times. That's a lot! We can help students by reusing language in different contexts or by returning to language in review lessons. This also gives us the opportunity to check their learning.

Monitoring learning

Another very immediate way of assessing learning is monitoring. When students are working in pairs or groups, I always make sure I walk around the class to listen to them. It's the best way to make sure they are doing what I've asked them to do, as well as listen for the language they are producing.

Teacher Tip

The next time you monitor a task, note down which of the following things you discover:

- Some students didn't know what to do.
- Everybody was interested in the task.
- Some students weren't doing the task.
- You were impressed by the language some students used.
- You found some students making errors.

All of these points will help to inform your future teaching.

Sometimes we monitor very openly by moving around the classroom and listening to or looking at what students are doing. This gives us the opportunity to refocus students back to a task if they are getting side-tracked and to encourage everyone to participate. But sometimes I will monitor from a distance to give students some space to work without feeling any pressure. It depends on the class and the lesson I'm teaching.

Feedback

When we assess learning it gives us information to use as we continue teaching and allows us to give feedback to our students – not only positive feedback but also things they need to think about more. Positive feedback is just as important as telling our students how to improve. Positive feedback is an important tool for motivation. But even the best student can improve, and wants to improve, so we should always include something for them to focus on. It's equally important to recognise the effort they have made in their studies. Traditionally, we have thought of feedback as something that we provide to students. But have you ever thought about asking students to give feedback to each other, or to feed back on their own learning? In Chapter 6 **Active learning** and Chapter 8 **Metacognition** we talk about how we can help students take more responsibility for their learning by making them more active. So, if they are thinking about feedback, either for themselves or for their classmates, this is active learning, too. We pass some of the responsibility for their learning to them. This in turn makes them more independent and better language learners.

Let's look at the different sources of feedback.

Teacher feedback

We sometimes give feedback to a whole class after an activity, or to comment on a whole lesson.

Teacher Tip

Look at the following short pieces of feedback that teachers have given. Think about them from the students' perspective. How would these make you feel?

1 Well done, everyone! You did that speaking activity perfectly. It's the best work you have ever done.
2 Your writing homework last week was really interesting. Thank you if you tried to use the new vocabulary we learnt last week. I'd like everyone to remember how we talked on Monday about checking work for spelling errors this week and to focus on that. I can't wait to read your stories.
3 Everyone made the same mistakes with prepositions in that exercise. I want you to spend some time this evening revising to make sure it doesn't happen again.

I'm sure we'd all agree that the last one isn't very encouraging. I've never found feedback like this to be motivating for students. In this example, telling students that they need to revise without telling them what they need to revise isn't likely to encourage them to do anything!

The first two examples of feedback are both positive. Example 1 will certainly make students go away feeling good about themselves. It will boost their egos but after that … what will happen? They don't know what to do to improve. This sort of feedback isn't very useful. However, I have used phrases like this with nervous students before an exam when their confidence needed a boost.

Example 2 has the best balance. It recognises what students have done by saying that their work was interesting, and also highlights students who have gone further than others using new vocabulary. Importantly, it gives students a focus for their next work and ends with encouragement.

If we are lucky, we can give individual feedback to each student about his or her work, but often with the number of students we teach this isn't practical. We do frequently give them written feedback on their written work and we need to make sure this is as useful as possible. I find giving students a mark for their work, which was sometimes necessary in the schools I have taught in, means they were only interested in the mark. Any comments that I added were often not read, let alone considered. Lesson idea online 7.1 provides an example of how I try to make sure students get as much as possible from feedback.

☑ LESSON IDEA ONLINE 7.1: FEEDBACK CODE: CAT TRANSFORMATION

This lesson idea focuses on giving feedback on written work using a feedback code (Figure 7.2). Here it is used in a piece of writing, but the same code can be used in any homework exercises. This exercise helps to familiarise students with the code.

✓	good language
Things to check ….	
Sp	spelling
T	tense
G	grammar
WO	word order
WW	word used
MW	missing word
X	extra word or words
C	capitalisation
P	punctuation
A	agreement, e.g. 3rd person s

Figure 7.2

You may decide to focus on one type of error on a piece of written work. This is particularly useful if there are a lot of errors to indicate. This will also let you look at different areas for different students, which is useful in recognising differences in your students. When students are familiar with this process, I give written work back and ask them to use the symbols to correct it, before they hand it in again. Only at this point do I give a mark, if required.

Teacher Tip

Students are often more keen to know what their errors are than I am, as the teacher, to focus on them. This is especially true when you are trying to focus on fluency rather than accuracy. You can avoid interrupting fluency-focused activities but still acknowledge this need for feedback on errors. I often share any errors I have heard while monitoring at the end of the lesson, or maybe at the start of the next one, and ask students to correct them. You may want them to do this individually first and then to share with a partner, or they can work with other students.

- Put errors on the board and tell students they are all things that you heard during the task.
- Ask them to look at each one and to find and correct the error, and also to think about why the error was made.

You could start this by reading out some *good* examples that you have heard, to make sure these are recognised, too.

It is important that students don't feel embarrassed by their errors so never identify who made them. Sometimes I change some of the words so that they are more anonymous, too.

For example: *I am the only person in the class who is interested to art, I think* could be changed to *He is the only person in the class who is interested to music, I think* without losing the error.

Between 10 and 15 errors is a good number to keep the students interested and to create a ten-minute activity.

Some people might wonder why we don't just correct the sentences ourselves. If our students do it themselves they are more likely to remember the corrections. This makes our students more active in their learning, as discussed in Chapter 6 **Active learning**. It is also an introduction to peer- and self-feedback. Although you have chosen the sentences to focus on, students are thinking about what the errors are as well as why they may have been made.

Student feedback

> **☑ LESSON IDEA ONLINE 7.2: WHAT COMES FIRST?**
>
> This is an activity that can be used for homework and leads into a peer-feedback task, which can be used as the warmer for the following lesson. It's adaptable to different levels and can be focused on specific language or be more open. It doesn't require a lot of teacher preparation and provides a wealth of information about students' approaches to their learning, as well as on the content of their work.

This activity demonstrates a simple and common technique that we all use – although we might not know that it has a name! Think–Pair–Share involves students working alone initially to think of their answers. They then join with another student to exchange their thoughts and to develop them based on what their partner says. Finally, they share their ideas in groups or with the whole class. It provides an opportunity for all students to contribute and time to consider their ideas, and encourages listening and reflection on a larger scale.

With self-feedback, you'll need to introduce the practice carefully and support or scaffold activities to make sure students realise the value of what they are doing. This isn't a quick process, but if we do it carefully then it sets really good practice for students in their learning. And of course this isn't just valuable for our subject: it is helpful in every subject.

Teacher Tip

Does your school have a policy on feedback? If so, does it include students giving each other feedback and self-feedback? Discuss this with teachers for other subjects. How can you work together to support this? If there isn't a policy, maybe you could suggest you all work together to produce one! Here are some ideas of things you should consider including:

- the whole school approach to feedback

- types of feedback – from the teacher, from other students or self-feedback
- when feedback should be given – in class, in feedback sessions, at the end of a lesson
- how feedback should be given – orally, short feedback in a workbook, more formal reports
- what is included in feedback – good feedback should include positive things as well as areas to work on. Many teachers use the 'two ticks and a wish' approach to highlight two positive areas and something for the student to work on to close the gap between their level and the desired level.

☑ LESSON IDEA ONLINE 7.3: SELF-ASSESSMENT FEEDBACK

This activity can be used with any type of lesson you teach and provides an opportunity for students to reflect on and record their learning. It's also helpful for us as teachers and lets us reflect on what has worked well and what we can improve on. You could ask students to do this for homework or give them time at the end of the week to complete it.

Assessment for Learning progress

Although Assessment **for** Learning is a vital part of our teaching toolkit, it doesn't mean that assessment **of** learning isn't useful too. There is often a progress check or test at the end of each unit of a coursebook. The fact that it is called a 'test' doesn't stop it being used to encourage more learning. In fact, the least useful application of these tests is just as a test to produce a number of correct answers. One thing that such stand-alone tests never show is progress. A student who consistently gets everything correct on such a test, but who gets only three-quarters correct on one particular test, will need different feedback from another student who doesn't usually do well, but who gets the same three-quarters correct. In this case, 75% will be a very impressive outcome and should be recognised.

Most schools also have some sort of summative assessment at the end of the school term or year. You may be able to give students back their test papers to look at, although not all schools allow this. In either situation, what the students spend their time on in the test gives you lots of information to use formatively to influence your teaching. If students are able to look at their own test papers, they can incorporate what they did well and what they need to improve on into their feedback reports using the traffic lights system as described in Lesson idea online 7.3. If it's not possible to give papers back then you will have to do slightly more work to extract this information – it is too valuable to be lost as just a number of marks or a percentage mark for a test.

Summary

Now that we've looked at Assessment for Learning, you will have a good understanding of:

- when we use Assessment for Learning and why

- using questions effectively

- monitoring your students while they work

- how students can use feedback from teachers and classmates and can self-assess

- using summative assessments to help students in their learning.

8 | Metacognition

What is metacognition?

Metacognition describes the processes involved when students plan, monitor, evaluate and make changes to their own learning behaviours. These processes help students to think about their own learning more explicitly and ensure that they are able to meet a learning goal that they have identified themselves or that we, as teachers, have set.

Metacognitive learners recognise what they find easy or difficult. They understand the demands of a particular learning task and are able to identify different approaches they could use to tackle a problem. Metacognitive learners are also able to make adjustments to their learning as they monitor their progress towards a particular learning goal.

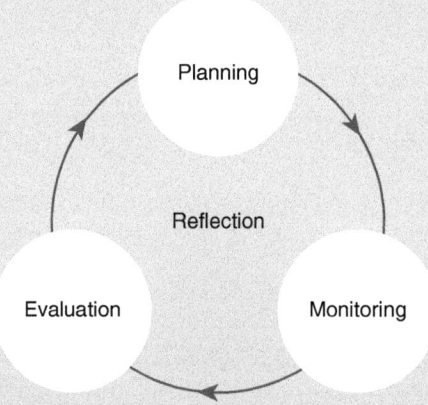

Figure 8.1: A helpful way to think about the phases involved in metacognition.

During the *planning* phase, students think about the explicit learning goal we have set and what we are asking them to do. As teachers, we need to make clear to students what success looks like in any given task before they embark on it. Students build on their prior knowledge, reflect on strategies they have used before and consider how they will approach the new task.

As students put their plan into action, they are constantly *monitoring* the progress they are making towards their learning goal. If the strategies they had decided to use are not working, they may decide to try something different.

Once they have completed the task, students determine how successful the strategy they used was in helping them to achieve their learning goal. During this *evaluation* phase, students think about what went well and what didn't go as well to help them decide what they could do differently next time. They may also think about what other types of problems they could solve using the same strategy.

Reflection is a fundamental part of the plan–monitor–evaluate process and there are various ways in which we can support our students to reflect on their learning process. In order to apply a metacognitive approach, students need access to a set of strategies that they can use and a classroom environment that encourages them to explore and develop their metacognitive skills.

Why teach metacognitive skills?

Research evidence suggests that the use of metacognitive skills plays an important role in successful learning. Metacognitive practices help students to monitor their own progress and take control of their learning. Metacognitive learners think about and learn from their mistakes and modify their learning strategies accordingly. Students who use metacognitive techniques find it improves their academic achievement across subjects, as it helps them transfer what they have learnt from one context to another context, or from a previous task to a new task.

What are the challenges of developing students' metacognitive skills?

For metacognition to be commonplace in the classroom, we need to encourage students to take time to think about and learn from their mistakes. Many students are afraid to make mistakes, meaning that they are less likely to take risks, explore new ways of thinking or tackle unfamiliar problems. We as teachers are instrumental in shaping the culture of learning in a classroom. For metacognitive practices to thrive, students need to feel confident enough to make mistakes, to discuss their mistakes and ultimately to view them as valuable, and often necessary, learning opportunities.

Recognising successful language learning strategies

As we teach, we aim to make our students aware of what they learn, how they learnt it and how they can use this awareness in future learning. This makes them more successful at language learning than those who just focus on the outcome: the new language. We can help students who recognise where they have been successful in their language learning to apply similar strategies to future learning. Similarly, if a student finds a particular way of learning less successful, they can think about how to adapt this in the future so that they do better. In this chapter, we will look at what students can gain by having good metacognitive awareness, and the strategies they can use to improve and learn more.

Teacher Tip

Look at these statements from students. Which of them do you think show students who have an awareness of 'what they know'?

1 I hear English people using irregular verbs much more frequently than regular verbs.
2 English spelling is really hard to learn.
3 English speakers often squeeze some individual sounds so that you hardly hear them.
4 English speakers speak really quickly.
5 I never read a whole text without scanning through it first to see what it is about.
6 Phrasal verbs can have a literal and a non-literal meaning.

Students 1, 3, 5 and 6 are making observations about the language they are learning and have noticed a pattern or feature, or have realised that a particular approach to a task will help them to learn more effectively. The other two speakers, 2 and 4, are making an observation about the language but their statements don't show that they have noticed anything that will help them in their language learning. The other students are well placed to use their knowledge to help themselves learn more effectively.

Students who see patterns in language can use this ability to help spot other patterns later, or to see where something follows a different pattern. As we discussed in earlier chapters, when students break an activity into parts and prepare well for reading or writing tasks, for example, they are more likely to be successful.

When we consider metacognition we think about how we can help to move our learners from not just recognising such features but to being confident about how they can use them to improve their learning. So, they know what they need to do and they know how to do it, but they also understand why they could consider doing it in a particular way, or by using a particular strategy.

Research shows that students who are active in the planning, monitoring and evaluation of their own learning learn more and are more successful. The strategies that we can help them to acquire will make them more independent learners, too. Much language learning actually takes place outside the classroom – we can never aim to teach our students all of the English language that they will need in their lives. This is partly because their needs will change as they grow up and move into further education or the world of work. Also, the needs and interests of students are different. The more we can teach them about *how* to learn language, the more we are making sure they will be successful in the long term. In addition, it is very motivating for students to be able to work out the best way for them to learn personally.

There are five stages of how students use metacognitive strategies:

1 preparing and planning for learning
2 strategy selection
3 monitoring
4 planning strategy use
5 evaluation.

Preparing and planning for learning

You will see that in all the lesson ideas in this book the first stage always provides something to get students thinking about the task they are going to do. It might be a quick discussion with a partner or imagining what a text is going to be about. It doesn't need to be anything long or complex but, in real life, we never start to do anything without some expectation about what we are doing and why. Language learning should be the same. This first stage helps our students to activate any prior knowledge of the subject and the skills that they will need to be successful. But we can go beyond this. We know what our goals and aims are for a lesson and for different parts of a lesson, but how often do we share these with our students? There is no reason to keep this from them and if they know why they are doing something they are more likely to be engaged with it. For example, in a 'listening for gist' activity, you should tell students that they are listening to establish the main idea – you might have a simple question or a matching task as we saw in Lesson idea online 3.1 to help them to focus on this. Alternatively, you could ask students to set their own goal for this. Different students will have different strengths and areas to work on. Taking an example of a listening dialogue, here are some possible aims students could decide on:

- to identify what the relationship between the people talking is
- to identify where these people are
- to decide why the people are having the conversation
- to identify any words that link to the topic
- to identify the attitude of the people from their intonation.

Teacher Tip

We can't expect our students to be successful at identifying what they want to listen for without some training. To help students learn this self-selection skill, you could spend some time brainstorming different ideas such as the ones just mentioned and recording them for students to think about. If you have space to put these up on the wall in your classroom it will be a reminder for them for future reference.

After a 'listening for gist' activity, students can share the answers to their self-set question with their partners – this in itself will help students expand their view on what to select in the future.

An important feature of planning is for students to link back to previous experience. This might be previous experience of the language being taught or the skills and approaches used previously. Students are exposed to so much during their lessons that we can't expect them to do this automatically and we need to signpost this to help them. For example, when they have done a similar activity you could start the lesson by asking them to look back in their textbooks and think about how they did the task, what worked well, what they found most challenging and what they might have done differently. Of course, this will be different for different students.

Strategy selection

Throughout your teaching you will be giving students strategies for approaching a task. Making these strategies explicit and clear will help students remember them rather than just thinking about them as an instruction for a task. Strategies that have names will therefore be more memorable for our students.

Teacher Tip

Think about some of the strategies you have seen in the lesson ideas in this book as well as some you use in your teaching. Could you work with your students to give these strategies names? If your students work with you to name them, they will be more likely to remember them. For example, we might refer to students *deducing the meaning of new vocabulary in a text*, but my students named this strategy *looking for clues*.

Different students also have different preferences for the ways they do things. If we show them different ways and discuss these in class, it can help them to identify what they prefer and what they feel is more successful for them.

☑ LESSON IDEA ONLINE 8.1: BACK-TO-BACK LISTENING

This idea helps students to consider whether they prefer to take notes when listening or to listen without writing anything down. It works best with a listening text that contains factual information as well as opinion and can be used at different levels.

Lesson idea online 8.1 allows students to consider which listening method they prefer. In a lot of tasks students need to write things down, but there will also be opportunities for students to make their own choices. It is interesting for students who don't write to discuss how they keep their focus. For example: Did closing their eyes help? Does sitting on their hands make them less likely to move things on their desk and become distracted? These are examples of how they can think about how they learn best, e.g. metacognitive strategies.

Monitoring

While students are completing a task they need to be aware of how a strategy is working. For instance, if they are looking at unfamiliar vocabulary in a reading text, they might be trying to 'unpack' the word by identifying if there is a prefix that helps them to understand meaning and if there is a suffix to tell them what type of word it is.
For example:

prediction

- *pre-* tells them this word may have the meaning of 'before'. Other words they might know starting with the same prefix might help them to work this out.
- *-tion* tells them this word is probably a noun as this is a common way of turning verbs into nouns.

However, students might also look at the context in which the word is used and the surrounding 'sense' of the text to work out what it means. They may start with either strategy. Students who are very analytical are more likely to start by looking at the prefixes and suffixes, while students who prefer to take a more holistic view of a text may start by thinking about how the word fits with the context and structure of the text. Neither is better than the other and our goal in promoting metacognitive strategies is to make students aware of their use, and to consider which is more effective for them on any particular occasion. It is useful to have whole class discussions about these decisions and to get feedback to keep students aware of this, and to make sure they consider their choices.

Planning strategy use

Very aware students are able not only to think about the strategies they prefer and monitor how successful they are, but also to consider changing strategies while they are doing a task or activity.

Teacher Tip

To help your students to do this effectively you can highlight questions that students should ask themselves. This may mean that they make changes to the way they approach a task. Questions might include:

- Am I progressing with this task in the way I thought I would?
- Do I understand the language I am seeing?
- Is the language I am using making sense?
- Is there a better way of doing this task?

This takes the practice of self-monitoring a step further and students analyse what they are doing, making conscious adaptations to improve their learning.

Evaluation

It's very tempting for students to finish a task and then move straight on to something else. In some situations we may want them to do this if it is part of a series of tasks and the flow of the lesson depends on this. However, students need to be given an opportunity to evaluate how well their strategies for learning have worked. Eventually, we would hope that students do this automatically as they take more and more ownership of their learning. But it is also useful to give them the opportunity to do this more formally in class, or for homework, following an activity. The self-assessment feedback that we looked at in Lesson idea online 7.3 is one way you can capture this, but sometimes you may find it useful to get students to discuss the strategies that they have used with a partner in class, or you could ask students to contribute to a class blog on the theme of using strategies. The ability to reflect on learning is an important skill that will help our students to develop, and this will require classroom time.

Levels of awareness

Needless to say, developing the use of these strategies isn't something that will happen quickly, but it should be integrated into our teaching so that we gradually build awareness. Four levels of awareness of metacognitive strategies were identified by Perkins (1992), as shown in Figure 8.2.

Tacit ➡ Aware ➡ Strategic ➡ Reflective

Figure 8.2

At the beginning *tacit* level, students aren't aware of the strategies they are using. They will use whatever strategy they are told to use without thinking about what it offers them. Students who are *aware* have some knowledge of strategies but aren't usually very active in selecting them until prompted. Students who become *strategic* in their use are active and think about what strategies are most suitable and why. The ultimate goal is for our students to become *reflective*. This means that they take the time to consider what has worked well and what has not worked as well, and in doing this modify their approach for the future.

☑ LESSON IDEA ONLINE 8.2: PROCESS WRITING

This type of writing focuses on 'how' the writing process works – the end product is in many ways less important than getting your students to understand the process that they use for writing. This activity focuses on the writing process and provides an ideal opportunity to build metacognitive awareness.

Process writing is often an activity that is spread out over several lessons to avoid students getting bored of the topic or process. If students are aware of why they are spending more time than they might usually spend on a piece of writing, it is a very valuable activity.

What does this mean for classroom practice?

Teaching our students metacognitive skills is a process and one that we need to devote some time to. However, it doesn't need special technology or supporting material. It has a significant impact on learning and it won't cost our schools lots of money. And, of course, it is a part of making our students active in their learning, as we discussed in Chapter 6 **Active learning**.

Table 8.1 illustrates what teachers who focus on developing metacognitive skills will and will not say to their students.

Won't say ...	But will say ...
This is how to do this task.	How will you do this task?
Do this if you have a problem.	What can you do if you have a problem?
These are the answers.	What is your answer? How did you decide on that answer?
We've done this before.	When we did this sort of activity before, how did you do it?

Table 8.1: Examples of how teachers phrase things metacognitively.

Teacher Tip

Another useful teacher tool is to talk through how you might approach a task by 'thinking aloud'. This is a very useful way for students to understand the concept of thinking about learning. An ideal opportunity to do this is when activities have an example as the first item.

For example, in a listening task about jobs that people choose:

What is important to me as a job? I will listen to hear if these things are mentioned. Looking at any pictures of the people in my coursebook, how old are these people? What jobs can I imagine them doing?

If the task has an example, you could play the first part of the recording to allow students to check their predictions against this example before moving on.

☑ LESSON IDEA ONLINE 8.3: DIALOGUE BUILD

In this lesson idea students work as a class to practise a spoken dialogue. This lesson incorporates metacognitive strategies throughout. You can also get students to evaluate the activity and talk about how they did it afterwards. For this activity you will need a clear space on the classroom floor to lay out the dialogue build cards.

A final thing we need to remember is that, although the five stages of metacognitive thought are often shown as a process, with students moving from one to the next, in reality students will move backwards and forwards as they need to in order to complete a task successfully. In fact, being able to do this probably means they have internalised the concept and process and have built it into their language learning practice.

Summary

Having considered metacognition, you now know that:

- it is something that students should understand
- we need to spend time focusing on metacognition in our lessons
- there are different stages of thinking metacognatively
- it helps students to be more successful learners – of language and other subjects.

Language awareness

9

What is language awareness?

For many students, English is an additional language. It might be their second or perhaps their third language. Depending on the school context, students might be learning all or just some of their subjects through English.

For all students, regardless of whether they are learning through their first language or an additional language, language is a vehicle for learning. It is through language that students access the learning intentions of the lesson and communicate their ideas. It is our responsibility as teachers to ensure that language doesn't present a barrier to learning.

One way to achieve this is to support our colleagues in becoming more language-aware. Language awareness is sensitivity to, and an understanding of, the language demands of our subject and the role these demands play in learning. A language-aware teacher plans strategies and scaffolds the appropriate support to help students overcome these language demands.

Why is it important for teachers of other subjects to be language-aware?

Many teachers are surprised when they receive a piece of written work that suggests a student who has no difficulties in everyday communication has had problems understanding the lesson. Issues arise when teachers assume that students who have attained a high degree of fluency and accuracy in everyday social English therefore have a corresponding level of academic language proficiency. Whether English is a student's first language or an additional language, students need time and the appropriate support to become proficient in academic language. This is the language that they are mostly exposed to in school and will be required to reproduce themselves. It will also scaffold their ability to access higher order thinking skills and improve levels of attainment.

What are the challenges of language awareness?

Many teachers of non-language subjects worry that there is no time to factor language support into their lessons, or that language is something they know little about. Some teachers may think that language support is not their role. However, we need to work with these teachers to create inclusive classrooms where all students can access the curriculum and where barriers to learning are reduced as much as possible. An increased awareness of the language needs of students aims to reduce any obstacles that learning through an additional language might present.

This doesn't mean that all teachers need to know the names of grammatical structures or need to be able to use the appropriate linguistic labels. What it does mean is that we all need to understand the challenges our students face, including their language level, and plan some strategies to help them overcome these challenges. These strategies do not need to take a lot of additional time and should eventually become integral to our process of planning, teaching and reflecting on our practice. We may need to support other teachers so that they are clear about the vocabulary and language that is specific to their subject, and how to teach, reinforce and develop it.

Language awareness within schools

For language teachers, 'language awareness' usually means having a knowledge of the workings of English: grammatically, lexically, phonologically and functionally. But in this chapter we will look at language awareness from the viewpoint of the whole school and the policy our schools set out on how language is used in the school as a vehicle of learning.

What is language policy?

Most schools set out their goals at a very high level in a statement that shows the long-term vision for the students. It is sometimes called a *mission statement* or *vision statement* and it is made public so that teachers, students and parents know what they can expect from the school. These statements show the sort of skills and values that the school hopes to encourage in its students. From these statements, schools set out their policies on different areas of student life. If we think about the school vision statement as the long-term aims for our students, then policies help us to see how we help them in achieving these aims. One of the most important areas for us as language teachers is the language policy. This may reflect the national language aims or the school's own particular language aims, or a combination of both, specific to your situation. It is a written, shared document that helps to guide teachers of all subjects, not just languages. A good language policy needs to be very practical. It will make sure that everyone in the school knows what is expected from them with regard to language.

So, what can we expect to find in a school language policy? Well, the language policy in my school will probably be different from yours because we are likely to be teaching in different schools with different aims. But firstly you should be able to see which language is used every day in the school for communication. It will also tell you which language different subjects are taught in. The policy should tell you how speakers with different mother tongues are supported in their learning, as well as how teachers who are teaching in a second language are supported. Of course, as English teachers we immediately think about the use of *English* in schools, but the language policy will make it clear what is expected for any other languages, too. This might be another language, which is spoken by all students in a bilingual situation, or other languages that are taught.

Teacher Tip

Find your school's language policy and note down the main areas it covers.

- Is the policy up to date?
- Do you think anything needs to be changed?
- Do you think anything needs to be added?

From our language policy, we can start thinking about language planning and the tools we can use to make this as effective as possible (see Figure 9.1).

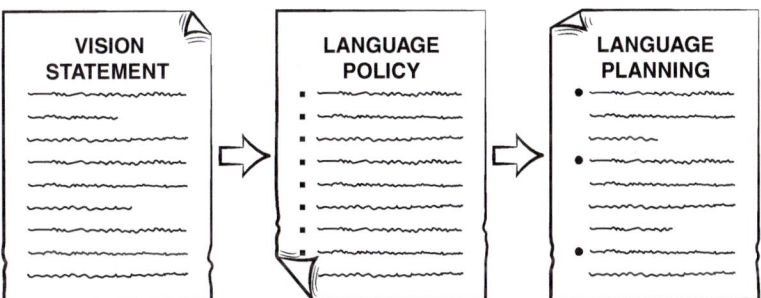

Figure 9.1

Teaching in English

If different subjects in your school are taught using English as the language of instruction, this an important area for you. This way of teaching isn't new and over the years it has had many different names. In some countries it is referred to as **CBI** – Content-based Instruction, **CBLT** – Content-based Language Teaching or **EAL** – English as an Academic Language. It is now most commonly referred to as Content and Language Integrated Learning, shortened to **CLIL**. The name is interesting as it shows that both the *subject content* and the *language* are important. It is more than just teaching a subject in a language. The two areas complement each other and the strength of CLIL is that both areas, subject-specific content and language, improve at the same time. Research has shown that when students learn in this way they are:

- more confident in their English skills as well as their first language skills
- able to remember and use a very wide range of vocabulary
- able to reach a higher level of English language proficiency
- more active cognitively during their learning.

CLIL is sometimes used from very early on – in primary schools, for instance – but it is more commonly introduced later, in secondary schools. In some schools, CLIL is used for certain subjects on a school curriculum, while others are taught in the students' first language. Subjects like History are sometimes taught in a first language as teachers feel there are strong cultural links. However, with a global perspective becoming more and more important in our schools, this is changing in some countries.

Students who learn through CLIL develop what are commonly referred to as '21st-century skills', such as being able to analyse and think critically about ideas and to evaluate their merit. In other subjects, students are able to think more creatively and can synthesise ideas that they learn.

However, without support and structure, studying in a second language environment is not likely to be successful. A researcher in bilingual education, Jim Cummins, made the distinction between two types of language skills:

- Basic Interpersonal Communicative Skills, or **BICS**, refer to the skills needed to communicate in everyday settings.

- Cognitive Academic Language Proficiency, or **CALP**, refers to the development of language for academic study. When they have developed this language our students can start to use the skills we talked about earlier, such as analysis and hypothesising.

Adapted from Cummins, J. (1979).

In the past, it was assumed that if a student had a good level of ability in BICS, they would automatically be able to learn the language they needed for the academic demands of CALP. We now know that this isn't the case and we need to make sure we give students the tools and skills they need to make this transition.

The 4Cs framework

CLIL can be explained using the 4Cs framework. As you can see from Figure 9.2, the 4Cs are set in the context of the subject and lesson being taught.

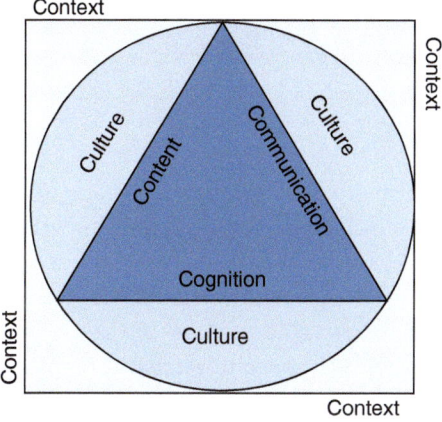

Figure 9.2

Culture

Here, culture means the setting of the lesson, whether that is local, national or global. One of the benefits of teaching using CLIL is that we can help our students to be aware of their place in the world and their responsibilities as global citizens.

We should also think about what CLIL *isn't*. It isn't only for the strongest students – it helps students of all abilities. It doesn't mean that the subjects need to be taught by a language expert, but it does mean that subject teachers need to build an awareness of language and how they use it. It doesn't mean that the subject content needs to be made easier. In fact, students can learn more as they develop more advanced cognitive skills.

When we think about the way we communicate globally now, being able to talk about subject content for Economics, Art or ICT, for example, is a big advantage for our students. They can read subject content on the internet in English and talk online to people studying the same subjects in other countries. This will really help them when they leave school and look for work.

The other 3 Cs sit within Culture.

Content

This refers to the subject content, whether that is looking at maps in Geography, how people breathe in Biology or business models in Economics. As English teachers, we need to consider this to see what language students need to know to be successful.

Communication

This is about how our students produce language in their subject lessons. We need to think about the skills (and sub-skills) in reading, writing, speaking and listening that students will need to communicate in their lessons. With strong communication skills, our students can interact in very meaningful situations, which is the ultimate goal for us all as language teachers. When we think about communication in CLIL we can break this down into three areas:

- Language *of* learning – language that is key to the specific content of that lesson, both lexical and grammatical. For example: key vocabulary for the lesson, conditional structures used for making suggestions.
- Language *for* learning – language the students need to take part in the lessons actively. For example, asking and answering questions and using language to build an argument.
- Language *through* learning – language that our students pick up and refine while using CLIL, for example from listening to other students' presentations or using dictionary skills.

Cognition

The last C is about how our students learn: which mental skills they are using. There are language demands here to consider from a functional perspective. If students need to use the skills of analysing then we need to equip them with the language to do this.

These three areas don't exist in isolation but provide different perspectives for us to think about as we support subject teachers and students in their lessons.

Teaching using CLIL

So, CLIL is clearly good news for our students. But what does it mean for us as teachers? It is certainly more than subject teachers just changing the language they use in the classroom. Subject teachers will need to think about the language they use to teach a particular area, and develop their understanding of why certain language might be challenging for students. Of course, colleagues in our schools who teach other subjects probably aren't language experts, so they are likely to need support in building this knowledge. We need to be aware of what each subject teacher has in their curriculum and when they plan to teach it.

Teacher Tip

Look at these examples from different subjects. Think about the language our students will need to be able to take part actively in these subject lessons.

- First, the impact of the war between the two countries was felt by the population. (History)
- If you add this chemical to the test tube, what will happen? (Chemistry)
- First you plot the two coordinates on the graph and then you multiply them by two to find the new position. Next, transfer the results to the chart. (Mathematics)
- Red blood cells pass through the lungs and take in oxygen. (Biology)

In these examples, we can see that students need to know the passive voice for History, conditional forms for Chemistry, sequencing words for Mathematics and present simple for Biology. But these are just four examples concerning a few subjects! There is clearly a lot for *us* to think about when our colleagues are teaching using CLIL. We may need to teach functions and grammar in a different order to how they are presented in our coursebooks, for example. This shows us how important it is for us to work closely with teachers who use English to teach their subjects.

Imagine the Chemistry teacher has told you that she is about to introduce the idea of mixing different chemicals and the reactions they produce. She needs to be sure that the class will be able to focus on the chemistry and will be able to produce the relevant grammar. She is going to ask the students to predict and imagine what will happen when different chemicals are mixed. As language teachers we will recognise that students will need to use the language of predicting what will happen and the first conditional. Lesson idea online 9.1 contains an activity you could use to review the first conditional to prepare them for this.

☑ LESSON IDEA ONLINE 9.1: FIRST CONDITIONAL LISTENING

This idea focuses on first conditional 'if' sentences, which students will need to use for talking about possibilities of things happening. This is useful language in many different subjects, including Sciences, Geography and Economics, for thinking about how two ideas are linked.

In other situations, you may recognise that a particular function is needed, for example speculating with various degrees of certainty.

☑ LESSON IDEA ONLINE 9.2: WHAT IS IT?

This speaking activity provides practice in the language needed to express certainty.

CEFR: what's it all about?

One of the most useful tools we can use to help us support subject teachers in the use of CLIL is the **Common European Framework of Reference**, or **CEFR**.

We can use the CEFR to judge the level of our students as well as the language that we are teaching them. It isn't a methodology and it won't tell you *how* to teach something. However, it will help you think about the needs of your students and how you can help them to develop the skills they need for their lessons.

The CEFR was produced by the Council of Europe to give a common standard that we can use across different languages in different situations. It thinks about the communicative skills of language: reading, writing, speaking and listening. There are six levels of language ability overall, as illustrated in Figure 9.3.

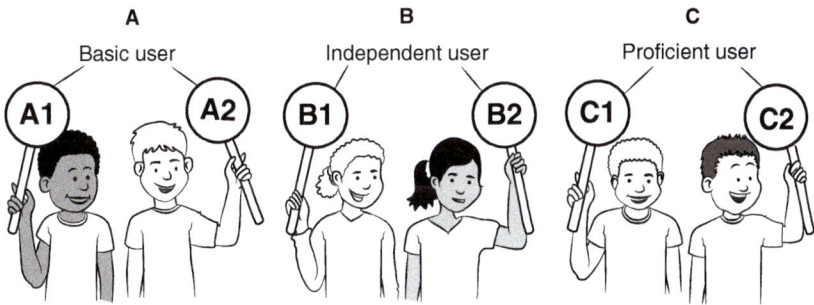

Figure 9.3

A1 is the lowest level of proficiency and C2 is the highest.

If we know what a student at a particular level is expected to be able to do, this allows us to check the level of our students against the CEFR.

Can Do statements

One of the most useful things about the CEFR for us as teachers is its *Can Do statements*. These describe what students at a certain level can do in certain situations.

To understand what these statements are, we can look at some examples from the *Can Do statements* that students use for self-assessment.

Teacher Tip

The following are *Can Do statements* for writing and give examples of the sorts of texts students can produce:

A2: I can write short, simple notes and messages.

B2: I can write personal letters describing experiences and impressions.

C2: I can write complex letters, reports or articles which present a case with a logical structure.

As you can see, the things that a student can do in these texts get more difficult as they move up the CEFR scale.

You can find the CEFR on the Council of Europe website, along with useful background information.

Once we decide what our students can do, we can look at what we expect them to be able to do and make sure we think about how to close any gaps. This is even more important when we think about teaching with CLIL. We can use the *Can Do statements* to think about what subject teachers want students to do in their lessons, and also to think about the level of our students to decide whether it is achievable. It may be necessary to talk to subject teachers about scaffolding their lessons so that students are supported and can build towards a task in stages. You can read more about this in Chapter 10 **Inclusive education**. This will help to make sure students can focus on the content of the lesson and won't feel put off by being asked to do a task that they aren't yet prepared for linguistically. Subject teachers might use visuals to show ideas, or break a task down into smaller stages, or ask students to work together on some parts of a task. The *Can Do statements* from the CEFR will help subject teachers to see where this might be necessary.

The English Profile database

The CEFR not only acts as a useful tool to use with other subjects that are being taught in English but can also be helpful in our own teaching. There are two very valuable resources that we can use to help us decide on the level of language to use:

• the English Grammar Profile
• the English Vocabulary Profile.

They can both be accessed through the English Profile website.

These resources are based on a huge corpus of student language, which has been collected over many years and analysed. There are examples from students all over the world, making it very useful to us as teachers. They both work in the same way and allow you to both check the level of certain language against the CEFR and look for language that fits certain criteria. Figure 9.4 is a screenshot taken from the English Vocabulary Profile and shows the results from a search on 'adjectives ending in -*ing*' at B1 level.

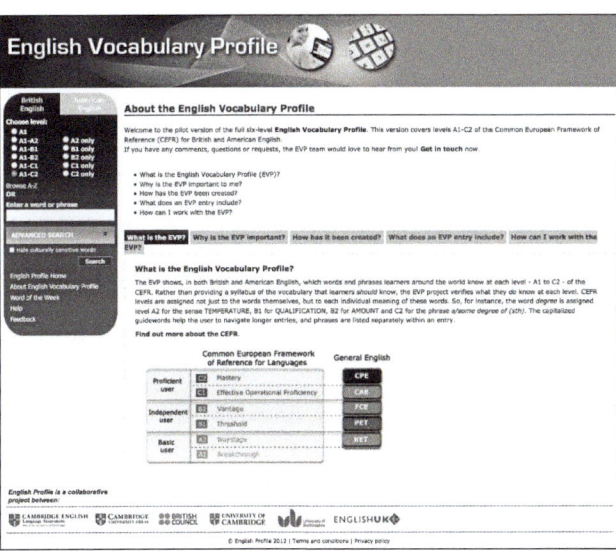

Figure 9.4

You can use these results to plan a lesson teaching adjectives, or check that adjectives used in an activity are within the level of your students. This tool is very useful if you think students will be working above their CEFR level in another subject. It helps you to predict what they may not know and gives you the chance to pre-teach any necessary language. You can find out more about how the English Profile works on its website.

Teacher Tip

It is often very motivating to use material that hasn't been specially adapted for language students in our classrooms. This could be newspaper or magazine articles, information from the internet or even TV and radio recordings for listening material. It's encouraging for students to know that they can learn from this authentic material. On the English Profile site you can paste in a text and get feedback on the level of the language, which can be very helpful if you want to plan a lesson around such material.

None of these tools, the CEFR or the English Profile databases, will tell us *how* to teach something, but they are very useful in helping to guide us in *what* to teach.

Summary

Now that we've looked at language awareness, you will have a good understanding of:

- The CEFR and the English Profile, and how we can use these to help our teaching.

- The use of English in the classroom for other subjects and how we need to support this.

Inclusive
education

10

What is inclusive education?

Individual differences among students will always exist; our challenge as teachers is to see these not as problems to be fixed but as opportunities to enrich and make learning accessible for all. Inclusion is an effort to make sure all students receive whatever specially designed instruction and support they need to succeed as learners.

An inclusive teacher welcomes all students and finds ways to accept and accommodate each individual student. An inclusive teacher identifies existing barriers that limit access to learning, then finds solutions and strategies to remove or reduce those barriers. Some barriers to inclusion are visible; others are hidden or difficult to recognise.

Barriers to inclusion might be the lack of educational resources available for teachers or an inflexible curriculum that does not take into account the learning differences that exist among all learners, across all ages. We also need to encourage students to understand each others' barriers, or this itself may become a barrier to learning.

Students may experience challenges because of any one or a combination of the following:

- behavioural and social skill difficulties
- communication or language disabilities
- concentration difficulties
- conflict in the home or that caused by political situations or national emergency
- executive functions, such as difficulties in understanding, planning and organising
- hearing impairments, acquired congenitally or through illness or injury
- literacy and language difficulties
- numeracy difficulties
- physical or neurological impairments, which may or may not be visible
- visual impairments, ranging from mild to severe.

We should be careful, however, not to label a student and create further barriers in so doing, particularly if we ourselves are not qualified to make a diagnosis. Each child is unique but it is our management of their learning environment that will decide the extent of the barrier and the need for it to be a factor. We need to be aware of a child's readiness to learn and their readiness for school.

Why is inclusive education important?

Teachers need to find ways to welcome all students and organise their teaching so that each student gets a learning experience that makes engagement and success possible. We should create a good match between what we teach and how we teach it, and what the student needs and is capable of. We need not only to ensure access but also make sure each student receives the support and individual attention that result in meaningful learning.

What are the challenges of an inclusive classroom?

Some students may have unexpected barriers. Those who consistently do well in class may not perform in exams, or those who are strong at writing may be weaker when speaking. Those who are considered to be the brightest students may also have barriers to learning. Some students may be working extra hard to compensate for barriers they prefer to keep hidden; some students may suddenly reveal limitations in their ability to learn, using the techniques they have been taught. We need to be aware of all corners of our classroom, be open and put ourselves in our students' shoes.

Inclusion in the language classroom

As discussed earlier in this book, English is a world language and the opportunities that it offers students are endless. We need to do our best to make sure that every single student in our class is able to reach their full potential in the subject so that they can then go on to do their best after their education finishes. This will involve thinking about how we can include everyone in classroom activities and how we can allow them to participate fully. Providing interesting lessons that are fun and that motivate students is central to this, of course. But we also need to recognise that not everyone learns in the same way or at the same pace. We might need to make some adjustments to the way we teach to make sure we are as inclusive as possible.

Differences

Although we plan our lessons for a class as a whole, we need to remember that each student is different. There are obvious differences that we discover as we teach them, like their interests and attitudes to language learning, but there are also less obvious differences that we need to be aware of. They might be related to the way they like to learn and process information, and in particular language. Students might be different because of behavioural and emotional factors. Sometimes, we will have students in our classes who struggle to keep their concentration on the language we are covering over longer periods of time, or who are distracted by their surroundings more easily in speaking activities, for example. Other students may have sensory or physical needs that we need to consider when we think about the skills we include in our lessons. There is no reason why students with visual or hearing impairments can't learn a language but, obviously, we will need to adapt activities and tasks to make them accessible to them.

Your school should have a policy to support you in these situations. This will help you to draw on resources or possibly teaching assistants who can help you in class. For some situations there may be invaluable specialist support and research to help you in making adjustments to your teaching. For other situations, careful thought about how you organise both the physical surroundings in your classroom and your lessons can make sure that your teaching is as inclusive as possible.

Let's look at how types of differences impact on our teaching and how we can help students in class.

Cognition

As discussed in Chapter 6 **Active learning**, students may have different styles that they prefer to use for learning.

Teacher Tip

Look at this list and think about how each one could be helpful to different students in your class.

1 roleplay
2 using timelines on a board to show the use of tenses
3 using a voice recorder to record a text
4 tracing words with their finger as they are spoken
5 making mind maps to show the relationship between words
6 repeating a new word over and over again when they learn it
7 using flashcards with pictures to show the meaning of words.

If we think about how we can include as many individual preferences as possible we will help to make our classrooms inclusive.

▣ LESSON IDEA ONLINE 10.1: STRIP CONVERSATION

This activity is a good example of where the needs of different students can be incorporated. The task includes speed writing as feedback, as well as strongly encouraging active learning and supporting analysis of metacognitive strategies.

Students who have specific cognitive needs which have been identified may need targeted support in your lessons. You should make sure you discuss these with the person in your school who coordinates this area.

Dyslexia, or word blindness as it is also referred to, is something to consider for language students. There is interesting recent research that suggests students can be dyslexic in one language but not necessarily in another. A Chinese neuroscientist, Li Hai Tan, found this to be particularly true if the first language doesn't use a writing system similar to English, e.g. Chinese or Korean. The lesson for us to take from this research is not to assume that a student who is or isn't dyslexic in their first language will be the same in English, or any other language they learn.

Teacher Tip

Dyslexic students need support when they look at written text. For example, they may find copying from the board challenging and they may record things incorrectly, which can have a negative impact on their learning. There are strategies we can use to support these students:

- You can provide a printout of any board work.
- When you use texts in class, the use of a coloured plastic transparency can help some dyslexic students.

Figure 10.1

- You could use different coloured text for alternate lines to help the words stand out. Reading black text against a white background makes reading harder for some dyslexic students.
- Some students with dyslexia find it more difficult to write on white paper so giving them coloured paper could help.
- For severe issues, there are alternatives to using the written word: students could use audio recordings, pictures or mind maps, for example.

The more ideas we can think of to present language to students, the more likely we are to give them something that works for them.

Behaviour and development

Students with needs in this category may have difficulty in remembering information or keeping their focus on what you want them to do. In more severe cases, they may have been diagnosed with ADHD (Attention Deficit Hyperactivity Disorder), in which case you should be given specialist support for your teaching.

In situations where students struggle to concentrate, you should think very carefully about how you give instructions for a task. Overloading a student can be very off-putting for them and can cause anxiety. In turn, this means they aren't able to do their best using the language you want them to focus on. There are strategies for giving instructions that will help any student who feels overwhelmed by a task for whatever reason, and these should be something to consider in any class. One approach could be to decide to write instructions for a task on the board as a record for them, or you could break the task down into smaller chunks and only give instructions for one part of a task at a time. Concept-checking to ensure that students have understood what to do is also helpful and provides confirmation that students are doing what you want.

Similarly, changing the focus in the classroom regularly will help these students to keep their focus for longer. Shorter stages in an activity that involve different skills are more likely to be easier for these students to manage. Often they will do better in tasks that have a kinaesthetic or visual focus. Lesson idea online 10.2 combines both of these.

☑ LESSON IDEA ONLINE 10.2: PREPOSITIONS GAME

In this short activity students use Cuisenaire rods, which are blocks of different colours and lengths, to build something and use this to practise prepositions of place. It is a physical activity and can be made into a game that students find very engaging.

It might also be useful to think about what you already have on the walls of your classroom. It's great to have displays of work and useful lists for students to refer to, but this might be a distraction for some students. Keeping the front of the classroom organised and fairly clear will help all students to focus.

Communication

Communication is central to language learning, but some of your students may struggle with this. It might be difficult for them to communicate in written form, when speaking, or both. It may be because they are shy or under-confident in their language ability, or it could be due to conditions such as autism or Asperger's syndrome. None of these reasons should prevent students from learning English but, again, we need to think about how to adapt our teaching.

☑ LESSON IDEA ONLINE 10.3: CREATE A CHARACTER

Students who need support in communication often enjoy drama and this can be incorporated into your lessons. In this lesson idea students 'become' another character. This technique often gives students the freedom to relax and allows them to participate in the activity.

Students with disorders such as autism often struggle to deal with change and may need structure, order and clarity in their learning. Activating their prior knowledge on a topic is very important, so the first stages of lessons in which you introduce a topic will be vital for them. Students with autism are often strong at recognising patterns and so can be very good at grammar, which has a set structure (e.g. regular past tense endings). However, they may struggle with anything irregular, such as the many irregular past forms of verbs. They are often good mimics and this can be to their advantage when practising pronunciation and memorising lists of words. Nevertheless, they will probably still need help with understanding what intonation patterns mean or how to use words appropriately for a given situation.

Physical and sensory needs

These are possibly the first needs that we think about when we consider how to be inclusive. This is often because they relate to things we can see. It may be a student who has physical disabilities and who finds it hard to move around, a student who has limited hearing or one who is visually impaired.

If you have a student who cannot move around as easily as others, there are obvious things to consider, such as access to the classroom, but you will also need to think about any tasks that involve standing up and moving. In group work you can make sure the other students move to work with this student. However, I would not include any mingle activities, such as the one in Lesson idea online 3.2, if I had a student with such physical difficulties in my lesson. Although other students would be able to move and come to this student, it would make them stand out as different, which is something to be avoided if possible.

With students who have visual or hearing impairments it is important to understand the extent of their impairment, and to know of any specialist equipment that they have to help them in their studies. In some cases, there may be easy adjustments you can make to help these students. For example, you may be able to enlarge printed material, which would enable a student with poor sight to participate in class activities without any further help. Your classroom layout and management will be important, too. Students with a visual impairment will depend on their hearing more than others and so group activities, in which the class gets very noisy, may be more challenging. Students with a hearing impairment may need to sit centrally in the class so that they can hear as much as possible. Alternatively, a student who lip-reads would benefit from sitting where they can see as many of their classmates as possible to help with this.

Teacher Tip

It may seem that students who have hearing impairments can't participate in listening activities. Students who have some hearing will benefit from listening with headphones, which cut out surrounding noise. Students who have less hearing ability can work from transcripts of listening tasks, which are usually found in Teachers' Books. This doesn't mean they are purely reading as they will be recognising the features of spoken language, such as false starts, repetition and pauses. These are features you could focus on in lessons to support them.

Differentiation

Being able to use differentiation in your teaching will help you ensure that all students are included in your lessons.

Differentiation means:
- thinking about the interests, abilities and the learning profile of your students
- placing the students at the centre of the learning process
- thinking about having variations of tasks or different learning outcomes for different students
- providing a different learning environment for students (for example, having a quiet area with less stimulating material on the wall to avoid distraction)
- being flexible with how you teach and providing scaffolding or support where it is needed.

Differentiation doesn't mean:
- you can't use the same material for the whole class
- putting students into fixed ability groups (language students usually have a 'spiky profile' with different strengths in different skills)
- not being able to teach to a whole class
- providing an individual lesson plan for each student
- teaching to the demands of the majority of the class.

A valuable way of differentiating is to put students in groups to work and to adapt the task you set for each group.

Figure 10.2

Teacher Tip

To provide additional support in a reading comprehension activity you could differentiate the task by:

- Blanking out some of the grammatical words, such as adverbs that connect sentences, or prepositions, for stronger readers to fill in when they have finished the activity. It must still be possible to complete the comprehension task without these words.
- Providing a list of more challenging vocabulary for less able or confident readers to refer to, which will help them to focus on the task of reading for understanding without being distracted by unknown lexis.
- Asking different members of a group to focus on different parts of the reading, which they then discuss with others in the group. This supports those who need a regular change of focus in order to complete a task.

We need to remember that how a student feels about their learning can change from lesson to lesson, particularly as they make improvements and learn more. So, any groups you form should not be static.

On other occasions you may want to pair students with different strengths in order to take advantage of what each student knows. Students of different abilities working together can also be valuable. Peer teaching is very motivational and the stronger students benefit from reinforcing their knowledge as the weaker students learn from them. In addition, project work is an excellent way of allowing for differentiated learning as students can work in a group with different roles that fit their individual abilities, strengths and interests.

It is useful for students to choose which activity they work on, too. We all recognise that on some days we can feel more engaged and motivated in a lesson than usual. Allowing students to decide on the level that they work at, or the outcome that they aim for, makes students more active in their learning.

Reflecting on how students respond to our teaching is a vital skill for us as teachers and allows us to put the students at the centre of our planning and teaching. As we do this, we learn about the individuals that we teach and what they know about the language. We also observe what works best for each of them as well as what doesn't suit them. The more we know about our students, the more we will be able to provide them with tasks that suit each of them, regardless of any particular needs they have. In turn, this makes our classrooms more interesting, more successful and more inclusive for everyone.

Assessment support

If any of your students that have specific needs are taking external exams, it is important that your school contacts the exam board as early as they can to make sure the student can take the exam as fairly as possible. Generally, exam papers can be provided in different sizes, with larger fonts, or in formats designed for visually impaired students. Allowance can be made for those who have a physical disability in writing, for example they can dictate their answers to a scribe. Different coloured paper can be used for dyslexic candidates to ensure they can do their best in the exam. In some cases lip-read versions of listening tests are available, or candidates with a hearing problem may be given exemption from the listening part of an exam. It is important as well for students to practise these special arrangements prior to an exam situation.

Summary

Having considered inclusive education, you now know that:

- Our students have differences that impact on their learning that we need to consider.

- Differences are varied and can be due to factors that are obvious and we can see, or may be less obvious – that we can't see.

- We can adapt our teaching to ensure that all students are able to participate in our lessons by using differentiated learning.

- All students can reach their full potential as language learners with careful planning and consideration.

11 Teaching with digital technologies

What are digital technologies?

Digital technologies enable our students to access a wealth of up-to-date digital resources, collaborate locally and globally, curate existing material and create new material. They include electronic devices and tools that manage and manipulate information and data.

Why use digital technologies in the classroom?

When used successfully, digital technologies have the potential to transform teaching and learning. The effective use of technology in the classroom encourages active learning, knowledge construction, inquiry and exploration among students. It should enhance an existing task or provide opportunities to do things that could not be done without it. It can also enhance the role of assessment, providing new ways for students to demonstrate evidence of learning.

New technologies are redefining relationships and enabling new opportunities. But there are also risks, so we should encourage our students to be knowledgeable about and responsible in their use of technology. Integrating technology into our teaching helps prepare students for a future rooted in an increasingly digitised world.

What are the challenges of using digital technologies?

The key to ensuring that technology is used effectively is to remember that it is simply a resource, and not an end in itself. As with the use of all resources, the key is not to start with the resource itself, but to start with what you want the student to learn. We need to think carefully about why and how to use technologies as well as evaluating their efficiency and effectiveness.

If students are asked to use digital technologies as part of their homework, it is important that all students are able to access the relevant technology outside school. A school needs to think about a response to any 'digital divide', because if technology is 'adding value', then all students need to be able to benefit. Some schools choose to make resources available to borrow or use in school, or even loan devices to students.

Safety for students and teachers is a key challenge for schools and it is important to consider issues such as the prevention of cyber-bullying, the hacking of personal information, access to illegal or banned materials and distractions from learning. As technology changes, schools and teachers need to adapt and implement policies and rules.

One of the greatest pitfalls is for a teacher to feel that they are not skilled technologists, and therefore not to try. Creative things can be done with simple technology, and a highly effective teacher who knows very little about technology can often achieve much more than a less effective teacher who is a technology expert. Knowing how to use technology is not the same as knowing how to teach with it.

A principled approach to using technology

Language students can make use of so many different forms of digital technology nowadays and this is a positive thing. There aren't many of us who don't use technology of some sort in our classrooms. However, there are some important questions that we need to ask ourselves to make sure we use it in the best way to support our students' language development.

So, what exactly do we mean by a principled approach? Well, the question that is central to this is:

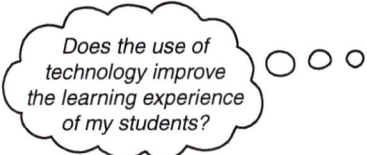

Does the use of technology improve the learning experience of my students?

It might seem like a strange thing to ask, but we need to make sure we place pedagogy ahead of technology. Language educators have talked about the *Everest Syndrome*. This comes from the answer one of the first men to climb Mount Everest, a British explorer called George Mallory, gave when he was asked why he had done it: 'Because it's there.' We need to make sure we don't use technology just because it is there, available to us and potentially appealing to students. If we don't think it actually helps the learning process, maybe it isn't the right choice. If it takes students longer to work out how to use an app or to navigate through a website, unless they are using English to do this, then it might mean that time isn't being well spent. In short, technology should work *alongside* more traditional ways of teaching and learning. If we ask ourselves key questions as we think about using technology to improve the language learning experience, we can make sure this happens and can use technology creatively to help our students:

- What technology can we use?
- Why should we use technology?
- How should we use the technology?
- Where and when should we use technology?

Using technology is a skill in itself and we don't all feel confident about using it in our lessons. It's usual to think about how we can start to develop skills, though, and how we can develop our expertise in using it. A useful model for thinking about this is **SAMR: Substitution, Augmentation, Modification, Redefinition** as shown in Figure 11.1. This shows an example of how a task can change as it moves through the levels shown in the boxes on the right.

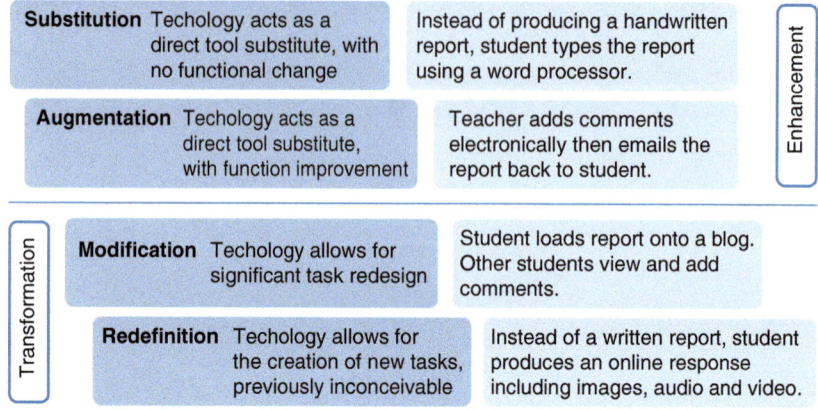

Substitution Techology acts as a direct tool substitute, with no functional change — Instead of producing a handwritten report, student types the report using a word processor.

Augmentation Techology acts as a direct tool substitute, with function improvement — Teacher adds comments electronically then emails the report back to student.

Enhancement

Modification Techology allows for significant task redesign — Student loads report onto a blog. Other students view and add comments.

Redefinition Techology allows for the creation of new tasks, previously inconceivable — Instead of a written report, student produces an online response including images, audio and video.

Transformation

Figure 11.1

In the top two layers of Figure 11.1 you can see that technology is introduced (Substitution) but is being used as a direct alternative for non-digital teaching – perhaps taking advantage of the more minor advantages that it offers (Augmentation). These are labelled 'Enhancements'. The bottom two layers show how using technology becomes transformational, completely changing the way in which we teach. Modification takes Augmentation a step further, and Redefinition allows for the creation of completely new tasks, which couldn't be implemented without the use of technology.

What technology to use?

We don't always recognise what type of technology we can use in our classrooms. Sometimes taking the time to think about the technology we use every day *outside* the classroom can help us to consider using it *in* the classroom to enhance learning.

Teacher Tip

Look at this list and tick the ones you currently use in your classroom.

news websites ☐	email ☐	mobile phones ☐
digital cameras ☐	podcasts ☐	electronic dictionaries ☐
social networks ☐	ebooks ☐	wikis ☐
interactive whiteboard ☐	webcams ☐	apps ☐
blogs ☐	data projectors ☐	presentation software ☐

Now look at the ones you haven't ticked. Could you use these as well?

This list isn't complete and there is a lot of hardware and software we can use, as well as considering the internet as a resource.

As mentioned in the section 'What are the challenges of using digital technologies?', we need to consider the safety of our students when we use certain resources, such as social media. However, there are ways we can help with this, such as creating password-protected blogs or making a Twitter account a closed group. Students need to be reminded not to share sensitive information as well. In practice, using social media in a more controlled way is an excellent approach to working cross-subject, reinforcing work done by ICT teachers.

☑ LESSON IDEA ONLINE 11.1: TWEETING

This lesson idea makes use of social media and the internet. Students don't need to access Twitter but you will need to find a suitable Tweet to use as a starting point. The Tweet should be appropriate for the age group of your students and relevant to their context. This activity works best with topics that are unusual and will interest students, and that aren't headline news at the moment.

107

Of course, not all of us have lots of resources like the things mentioned in the Teacher Tip above. That doesn't mean that we can't use digital technology at all. Just being able to access the internet, for example, gives us a wealth of resources that we can use. If we are creative, we can still integrate technology into our teaching.

Why use technology?

In language learning a very powerful reason for using technology is to allow students to use their skills to communicate with others. This might mean communicating with their classmates or other students in their school, but it could also mean students in other parts of the world. Our ultimate aim in teaching English is to equip our students to communicate in the real world. Why not start this in the classroom? Blogs are a good way to do this. Some teachers use blogs to communicate with their students, or to allow students to give feedback on their learning. This is a good introduction to the use of blogging for your students. Three types of blog are useful to consider as an introduction:

1 Teacher blog: owned by you as the teacher but students can post their comments on what you write. This is useful for giving whole class feedback in an informal way.
2 Student blogs: these are owned by individual students and they take control of the content but you can comment on their posts. This type of blog encourages students who may be less confident about giving their opinion in class, allowing them to share their feelings on their learning.
3 Class blog: this has shared ownership with anyone able to make posts and to comment. This type of blog is a good example of a Transformation in teaching according to the SAMR model we looked at earlier. Because they allow more than a one-to-one interaction pattern they can be considered a Modification task.

Teacher Tip

Sites such as Blogger and Wordpress allow you to set up blogs easily.

Using an interactive whiteboard (IWB) in class can really focus the whole class on a task. Even at the simplest level, if the students have read a text and completed a task associated with it, you can go through answers with the class using the IWB. As you get feedback you can highlight where in the text the answers are and go through any unfamiliar vocabulary as a class, highlighting the words.

☑ LESSON IDEA ONLINE 11.2: PRONOUN TRACKING

The IWB is a great tool for focusing on texts. This example shows how students can work together to analyse a text and look at the use of pronouns. You could also use this type of activity to focus on other features of discourse analysis, like the use of connectors such as *but, and, although*.

This activity is very visual and helps students to realise how frequently this feature of discourse is used. This can help to make them more aware of it when they are writing their own texts.

Tasks such as the one in Lesson idea online 11.2 can of course be done on paper, but using the IWB means feedback can be carried out effectively as a full class. As such, it is an example of Augmentation on the SAMR model. It isn't impossible to carry out the task without an IWB, but the task is improved for students with it.

If we use technology well, it can also be very motivating for students. It often appeals to students who sometimes don't engage with more traditional ways of learning. This can be particularly true for students with a preference for working visually. Highlighting how technology can be used can also encourage our students to be independent and see how they can use the resources around them outside the classroom.

☑ LESSON IDEA ONLINE 11.3: DICTIONARY QUIZ

In this activity, students use online dictionaries such as Cambridge Dictionary to solve questions in a quiz. The content of the quiz can be adapted to suit different levels and topics. The aim is to provide a fun way of promoting dictionary skills and student independence as well as different ways students can think about language.

It could be argued that this lesson idea is just a Substitution activity on the SAMR model. However, due to the wealth of information that online dictionaries offer, I feel it does much more than that and really augments it.

How to use technology?

We can think about technology in two ways: a resource to use in class and a resource to provide material to use in class.

The fact that so much of the internet is in English, though a lot of this hasn't been written for second language students, means that there is plenty of material we can download and use. YouTube and other similar sharing sites are popular with students and the content might be suitable and appropriate, but it might not be (make sure to supervise your students to ensure that they do not access any inappropriate content). It isn't a bad thing for students to be exposed to language that is above their level, particularly if it is a topic they are interested in, but we need to be careful in this area. There are plenty of sites that provide great material for us to access. These include BBC Learning English, which provides useful podcasts that are updated regularly. Searching for *Six minute English* will provide you with a listening file, the transcript, vocabulary that you may need to focus on, and the link to the original story on the BBC website. You can use these in class but I have also found that students often find these topics and resources useful for self-study. If you feel your students are enthusiastic about this, you could ask them to select one each to study for homework and report on in class. Many English language newspapers also have excellent resources aimed at language students. *The Guardian*'s Education section is one such example.

You can also find websites that have songs to use in the classroom, categorised by topic as well as the grammar they present. One such website is Tefl Tunes. Students often like learning English through songs and they can be a motivating way to introduce language.

As well as thinking about what resources we can find on the internet, we need to consider how we can use the tools we may have in our schools. One idea you might consider is using digital devices to let students record themselves speaking. This is one of the most valuable things that students can do and allows them to really focus on their speaking and pronunciation skills.

□ LESSON IDEA ONLINE 11.4: RECORDING SPEAKING

This activity requires students to record themselves having a conversation on a digital device such as a mobile phone or tablet. It highlights the differences in planned and unplanned speech as well as giving valuable listening practice.

It's clear that activities like this couldn't take place without using digital technology and so this is an example of a Redefined task on the SAMR model. The task has been designed around the use of the technology.

Where and when to use technology?

We've talked about fairly short tasks that involve using technology in the classroom. However, you can move beyond this and take advantage of access outside the classroom if this works in your particular context. Doing this opens up the opportunity to carry out a truly Redefined activity: project work. The topic and focus of any project work can vary, but scope is only limited by the resources available to your students. Some possibilities for project work include:

- Working individually or in groups.
- Doing shorter pieces of collaborative work, such as producing a monthly podcast about what has been covered over that period, or longer pieces that might last a whole term.
- Working in conjunction with students in other schools, or even other countries if a link school can be established – especially valuable if you are working in a monolingual context, as it adds a definite reason for speaking English and a level of interest.
- Using many different types of media to build elements of the project, for example video, digital pictures, web links, recordings and animation, as well as text.

- Working cross-curricular with other subject teachers to take a theme and consider it from different subject perspectives.

Project work opens the possibility for task-based learning. Students will need to know that a definite outcome is expected but there could be a high degree of flexibility in what is actually presented. This type of project work is highly collaborative and provides a very motivating way for students to work together in using their language skills.

IT policy

We talked in Chapter 9 **Language awareness** about the need for a language policy that sets out how language is used in your school. In the same way, your school should also have an IT policy. It is important to make sure that any activity you do in class with your students using digital technology, as well as anything you ask them to do out of class, falls within this policy.

From a principled approach to an integrated approach

When we take the principle that we talked about at the start of the chapter as our starting point, and then look at all the questions that we have considered since – what technology to use, why to use it, how it helps student learning, where and when it is most useful – the outcome will be an integrated approach. We will be using technology at its very best as a normal part of our teaching. It won't be seen as something different or special, and students will learn how they can be more independent in their language learning outside the classroom too. Advances in technology happen so quickly that this is an exciting area that will continue to develop and offer us exciting resources as language teachers.

Summary

Having considered the use of digital technology in the classroom, you now know that:

- We need to think about how using technology helps to achieve lesson aims.

- The SAMR model can help us to think about how we are using technology.

- We can think about using different software, hardware and internet resources in our teaching.

- When we have thought about all of these points, we can successfully integrate digital technology into our lessons.

12 | Global thinking

What is global thinking?

Global thinking is about learning how to live in a complex world as an active and engaged citizen. It is about considering the bigger picture and appreciating the nature and depth of our shared humanity.

When we encourage global thinking in students we help them recognise, examine and express their own and others' perspectives. We need to scaffold students' thinking to enable them to engage on cognitive, social and emotional levels, and construct their understanding of the world to be able to participate fully in its future.

We as teachers can help students develop routines and habits of mind to enable them to move beyond the familiar, discern that which is of local and global significance, make comparisons, take a cultural perspective and challenge stereotypes. We can encourage them to learn about contexts and traditions, and provide opportunities for them to reflect on their own and others' viewpoints.

Why adopt a global thinking approach?

Global thinking is particularly relevant in an interconnected, digitised world where ideas, opinions and trends are rapidly and relentlessly circulated. Students learn to pause and evaluate. They study why a topic is important on a personal, local and global scale, and they will be motivated to understand the world and their significance in it. Students gain a deeper understanding of why different viewpoints and ideas are held across the world.

Global thinking is something we can nurture both within and across disciplines. We can invite students to learn how to use different lenses from each discipline to see and interpret the world. They also learn how best to apply and communicate key concepts within and across disciplines. We can help our students select the appropriate media and technology to communicate and create their own personal synthesis of the information they have gathered.

Global thinking enables students to become more rounded individuals who perceive themselves as actors in a global context and who value diversity. It encourages them to become more aware, curious and interested in learning about the world and how it works. It helps students to challenge assumptions and stereotypes, to be better informed and more respectful. Global thinking takes the focus beyond exams and grades, or even checklists of skills and attributes. It develops students who are more ready to compete in the global marketplace and more able to participate effectively in an interconnected world.

What are the challenges of incorporating global thinking?

The pressures of an already full curriculum, the need to meet national and local standards, and the demands of exam preparation may make it seem challenging to find time to incorporate global thinking into lessons and programmes of study. A whole-school approach may be required for global thinking to be incorporated in subject plans for teaching and learning.

We need to give all students the opportunity to find their voice and participate actively and confidently, regardless of their background and world experiences, when exploring issues of global significance. We need to design suitable activities that are clear, ongoing and varying. Students need to be able to connect with materials, and extend and challenge their thinking. We also need to devise and use new forms of assessment that incorporate flexible and cooperative thinking.

The global language classroom

Many people say that the world has become smaller over the past 20 years as technology has given us access to so much global information. It's true that in the past it was sufficient to be familiar with our surroundings and our local context, but this is no longer the case. Our students will need to be prepared for adult life in a society that is multicultural and interdependent. If our aim in teaching English is to enable our students to be communicative members of this society in the 21st century, then it isn't enough to think about teaching them verb forms, vocabulary, pronunciation and so on. Our teaching needs to move beyond giving them reading and speaking practice in class. We need to give them the knowledge and skills to be able to be part of a global environment and to participate in it in their adult lives.

As a global language, English is an ideal medium to help with this. Unlike most other subjects, languages don't necessarily need to cover specific topics in their curricula. We generally aren't tied to a set list of topics that we need to include to make sure our students are prepared for exams and can move on to higher levels of study. This gives us the freedom to incorporate global topics and to promote the skills that support them.

To some extent, language teaching has aimed to do this for some time. As long ago as 1987 UNESCO's Linguapax project set aims that are very similar to those we think of when we consider global thinking nowadays. These include:

- to develop international understanding
- to promote international cooperation
- to promote better knowledge of world issues and concerns
- to enhance mutual respect and peaceful coexistence among people.

Global thinking in practice

These sound like huge aims, but as language teachers we can incorporate these into our teaching by considering global thinking. But what does this look like in practice? It isn't enough to think that if our coursebooks have topics that relate to other countries and cultures we have achieved this. Learning about how other people live is a good starting point, but we need to help our students to move beyond this so that they can engage in real global thinking. Some of the ideas that we've already talked about in earlier chapters are ideal for this, such as project work and creating blogs, but you can incorporate global thinking into any lesson by considering how local themes and topics can be enlarged and considered from different perspectives. This doesn't mean that our students can't think about themselves and that all topics need to be of worldwide importance. Global thinking is about enabling each student to see their place in the world.

Teacher Tip

Look at the chapter you are teaching in your coursebook. Can you identify the focus of the different activities? Which ones are:

- individual to the student?
- local?
- national?
- global?

You will probably find a mixture as many coursebooks are produced for global markets, which means they are varied and include many different perspectives.

It is useful to think about global education in four separate areas, as shown in Figure 12.1. We can then think about what each of these means for English and our teaching.

Figure 12.1

Knowledge

We can promote global thinking in our classrooms by including topics that will encourage our students to think about their place in the world and how other people live. The most common topics are related to social, political, environmental and economic issues. There are some huge issues relating to the environment, human rights, world hunger and how we live together. Using such topics, our students will learn how their actions relate to these areas and how they contribute to the lives of others. The phrase 'think global, act local' was first used in the 1970s when thinking about urban planning, but it is a useful way to think about the topic areas we can include in our lessons and the perspectives we want to help our students to develop.

Teacher Tip

There are many useful websites that provide up-to-date resources for you to use in your lessons. Global Dimension has links to good quality resources which come in a variety of forms. There are ideas for teachers to use as well as some ready-made lessons. A wiki produced by a magazine called *New Internationalist* has current topics and articles written in more accessible language. Again, there are whole lesson plans that you could consider using with your class as well as a useful search function to allow you to look for content on a particular global subject. The Breaking News website has articles on different topics and recent events in world news as well as a very useful feature that allows you to select the level of the content. There are four different versions of each article with useful activities at each level, including reading and listening input and ideas for focusing on grammar and vocabulary. There are also some really valuable activities where students rebuild a text they have read to focus on discourse features.

You'll find many of these topics in your coursebook, but we can consider any chapter of a book and think about how we can expand on the content to incorporate global thinking.

Teacher Tip

At lower levels, many coursebooks introduce basic verbs and adverbs of frequency that describe everyday events and times by asking students to describe what their routine is. For example, *I get up at 7am, I go to school from 9am to 4pm.* You can expand on this by asking students to choose a different country and find out about the school system there – they may find that students there have a different routine. It might be useful to do some preparation and ask students to research countries that have different school structures, for example places where they start school earlier in the day, where they go to school on different days or where they have longer or shorter school days. At higher levels, students can then speculate using modal verbs on how this impacts on life for these students and relate their routine to those of students in other parts of the world.

Grammar can be taught and reviewed using global issues. Thinking about the history, the present situation and the possible future situation of a global issue, such as pollution or climate change, gives practice in past, present and future forms. Comparative and superlative adjectives can be practised in these contexts, too.

There is also great scope for working across the curriculum with global topics. By linking what our students are doing in other subjects, we can make sure they recognise which language is relevant for their studies in these subjects if they are studying them in English.

21st century skills

We have already talked about the four language skills that our learners develop through their study: reading, writing, listening and speaking. Students will also need some other key skills, which are part of a set sometimes referred to as '21st-century skills'. This means that they are vital for our students to be able to compete in the global society that they will work in, using digital technology that is continuing to develop and change.

Four key competencies have been identified as part of these 21st-century skills: **critical thinking**, **communication**, **collaboration** and **creativity**. Let's look at each one individually.

Critical thinking

This refers to how students look at all the information available through traditional media and in digital forms, and evaluate it critically, weighing up different opinions and making informed judgements. Many tasks that we use in the language classroom require our students to solve problems and this is the first stage of critical thinking. We ask our students to deduce the meaning of unknown words that they find in a reading text, for example. We ask them to analyse how grammar is used when we use such tools as timelines and concept questions. We ask them to reflect on their own learning and consider what works well for them and what doesn't work so well. All of these are examples of thinking critically about language. Our students should then be well prepared to use these skills in activities and tasks that have a global element to them.

☑ LESSON IDEA ONLINE 12.1: CRITICAL EVALUATION

This lesson idea focuses on two different sources of information on one topic. It suggests using newspaper articles but other source material could also be used, for example blogs, wikis or even listening texts that you can find online. It helps students to think critically about what they read, but they also use the other three 'C's of communication, collaboration and creativity.

In Stage 5 of the lesson idea, students work together to produce comprehension questions. This is a particularly valuable exercise for students who are preparing for an exam and helps them to anticipate the skills and requirements of different tasks.

Communication

If our lessons are varied and active then communication is at the core of our classroom activities. But what do we mean by communication? Clearly, it includes speaking and writing, but we should also consider how our students communicate as well as how they will communicate in the future. Technology plays a big part in this. Speaking to somebody on the phone isn't the same as speaking to the same person face-to-face. Paralinguistic features and body language, such as hand gestures and facial expressions, mean that sometimes speaking on the phone is more difficult. Written communication by email is more similar to non-digital communication, but it is still important to consider how the reader will read our messages and whether they will understand what we want them to understand. Most communication that non-native speakers of English carry out is with other non-native speakers and our students are likely to need to work in diverse environments. A strong awareness of how our messages are understood is vital. As we all receive so much digital communication nowadays, we are often advised to keep messages brief and to the point. However, this can be challenging to do in a second language without sounding abrupt and rude and is an area that we can focus on with our students.

Teacher Tip

Getting students to email each other as part of a speed writing or functional lesson can be very good practice. If your school can set up some generic email addresses for you to use in class, this is useful. You can set up a situation, such as emailing a company for information about something, and pair students to be customer and company. Giving time limits for emails and responses keeps up the pace of this activity and provides lots of written language to review afterwards.

By including a variety of opportunities for students to communicate in class, we can integrate this element of global thinking into our lessons.

Collaboration

It's hard to think of any task or activity that is collaborative but that doesn't involve good communication. The two skills are closely linked.

Teacher Tip

Working collaboratively is important for learning, but so is having individual time for students to work alone. If your students are working alone it doesn't mean they aren't being active learners and it can provide them with time to plan contributions to collaborative tasks. It is good to have a balance in your activities. Look at your coursebook and think about the different interaction patterns the various activities suggest. How could you change them if you wanted to encourage more collaboration in class?

In the past in the workplace, people frequently worked alone at a job. It is much more common for us to work in teams now as the benefits of this are more widely accepted. It is the same in our classrooms. Students working in pairs or groups will benefit from the knowledge that their classmates bring to a task. Students learn how to work collaboratively from this as they have the opportunity to discuss, persuade, agree and disagree and, at times, compromise as they do activities. These are all key skills and we can provide meaningful practice in them in our lessons.

☑ LESSON IDEA ONLINE 12.2: FOOD SECURITY

This lesson idea focuses on a global topic but introduces the topic in a more personal manner with a listening exercise on food. The main activity is a dictogloss, which is where a text is read at normal speed three or four times. Students note down only the important words that will help them to reconstruct the text. In doing this, they focus on overall meaning, grammar, vocabulary and cohesion. They practise all four key skills as they do the task, as well as working creatively and in collaboration. It is a very valuable activity, but students need a gentle introduction to dictogloss if this is the first time you have used it. They may feel overwhelmed by what they think they need to do, so very clear instructions are essential.

Creativity in language processing

We have already talked about how successful language learners can see patterns in language and are creative when they try out new uses of language. This is a valuable skill and allows students to be innovative and to take risks. This is creativity in language processing. All teachers want to encourage creativity in their students. It allows students to take the subject further and show an interest in it. Despite any pressures we may have to cover the syllabus or to prepare our students for exams, we must make time for creativity in our teaching.

You can be creative in the classroom with some simple ideas that will encourage your students to try to do things differently, too. Here are some examples:

- Teach from the back of the class one day. It will give you a different perspective and will engage students.
- Change how you do activities. For example, give students the answers to a reading comprehension exercise and ask them to write the questions. This will give them a different perspective on the language.

We can encourage our students to be creative with simple activities that need very few resources. The most valuable resources, in fact, are our students and their imaginations!

☑ LESSON IDEA ONLINE 12.3: PAIRED CREATIVE WRITING

This is a fun activity which you can use with students of any level. It is very creative and also encourages communication and collaboration. It often produces unusual combinations of adjectives and nouns, which can lead to some very entertaining texts!

If you ask your students to be creative by doing something like singing a song or acting a part in a role-play, join in. This helps to foster a supportive atmosphere that is non-judgemental, and seeing you taking part will encourage them.

Global attitudes

Being able to consider the views and perspectives of others will help our students to have a better understanding of the world. Recognising that these may be due to different cultural factors helps them to move beyond this and develop a global attitude. A global attitude includes a respect for differences and diversity, a commitment to justice and an empathy with those whose lives are different from ours. Clearly, this is not something that can be taught quickly, or which students recognise instantly. However, incorporating global thinking into our teaching as a matter of course can help to achieve this.

Action

If we are successful in incorporating the knowledge and skills that we have discussed into our teaching, our students will be ready to be active members of a global community. Research has shown that businesses recognise the value of employing people who can think globally, are engaged and critical in their analysis of situations and can work in multicultural contexts. As a global language, English is ideally placed to help with this. Students who have a strong knowledge of global issues and can use the relevant skills collaboratively while using English to communicate will be valued in their future employment.

Summary

Having considered global thinking, you now know that:

- This is a key skill for our students in the 21st century.

- Thinking globally will help our students to consider other cultures and perspectives and to be active members of the global community.

- We can incorporate knowledge of global issues into our lessons.

- Our teaching needs to encourage the skills of critical thinking, communication, collaboration and creativity.

13 | Reflective practice

Dr Paul Beedle, Head of Professional Development Qualifications, Cambridge International Examinations

'As a teacher you are always learning'

It is easy to say this, isn't it? Is it true? Are you bound to learn just by being a teacher?

You can learn every day from the experience of working with your students, collaborating with your colleagues and playing your part in the life of your school. You can learn also by being receptive to new ideas and approaches, and by applying and evaluating these in practice in your own context.

To be more precise, let us say that as a teacher:

• You **should** always be learning
to develop your expertise throughout your career for your own fulfilment as a member of the teaching profession and to be as effective as possible in the classroom.
• You **can** always be learning
if you approach the teaching experience with an open mind, ready to learn and knowing how to reflect on what you are doing in order to improve.

You want your professional development activities to be as relevant as possible to what you do and who you are, and to help change the quality of your teaching and your students' learning – for the better, in terms of outcomes, and for good, in terms of lasting effect. You want to feel that 'it all makes sense' and that you are actively following a path that works for you personally, professionally and career-wise.

So professional learning is about making the most of opportunities and your working environment, bearing in mind who you are, what you are like and how you want to improve. But simply experiencing – thinking about and responding to situations, and absorbing ideas and information – is not necessarily learning. It is through reflection that you can make the most of your experience to deepen and extend your professional skills and understanding.

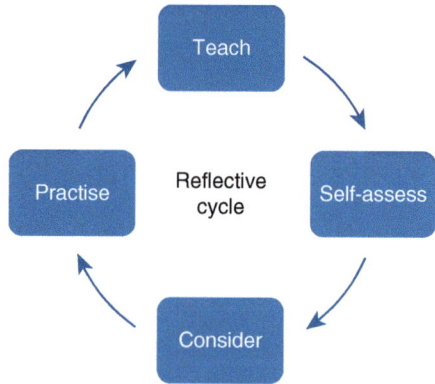

Figure 13.1

In this chapter, we will focus on three *essentials* of reflective practice, explaining in principle and in practice how you can support your own continuing professional development:

1 **Focusing** on what you want to learn about and why.
2 **Challenging** yourself and others to go beyond description and assumptions to critical analysis and evaluation.
3 **Sharing** what you are learning with colleagues – to enrich understanding and enhance the quality of practice.

These essentials will help you as you apply and adapt the rich ideas and approaches in this book in your own particular context. They will also help you if you are, or are about to be, taking part in a Cambridge Professional Development Qualification (Cambridge PDQ) programme, to make the most of your programme, develop your portfolio and gain the qualification.

1 Focus
In principle

Given the multiple dimensions and demands of being a teacher, you might be tempted to try to cover 'everything' in your professional development but you will then not have the time to go beneath the surface much at all. Likewise, attending many different training events will certainly keep you very busy but it is unlikely that these will simply add up to improving your thinking and practice in sustainable and systematic ways.

Teachers who are beginning an organised programme of professional learning find that it is most helpful to select particular ideas, approaches and topics which are relevant to their own situation and their school's priorities. They can then be clear about their professional learning goals, and how their own learning contributes to improving their students' learning outcomes. They deliberately choose activities that help make sense of their practice with their students in their school and have clear overall purpose.

It is one thing achieving focus, and another maintaining this over time. When the going gets tough, because it is difficult either to understand or become familiar with new ideas and practices, or to balance learning time with the demands of work and life, it really helps to have a mission – to know why you want to learn something as well as what that something is. Make sure that this is a purpose which you feel genuinely belongs to you and in which you have a keen interest, rather than it being something given to you or imposed on you. Articulate your focus not just by writing it down but by 'pitching' it to a colleague whose opinion you trust and taking note of their feedback.

In practice

- Plan
  What is my goal and how will I approach the activity?

  Select an approach that is new to you, but make sure that you understand the thinking behind this and that it is relevant to your students' learning. Do it for real effect, not for show.

- Monitor
  Am I making progress towards my goal; do I need to try a different approach?

  Take time during your professional development programme to review how far and well you are developing your understanding of theory and practice. What can you do to get more out of the experience, for example by discussing issues with your mentor, researching particular points, and asking your colleagues for their advice?

- Evaluate
  What went well, what could have been better, what have I learned for next time?

  Evaluation can sometimes be seen as a 'duty to perform' – like clearing up after the event – rather than the pivotal moment in learning that it really is. Evaluate not because you are told you have to; evaluate to make sense of the learning experience you have been through and what it means to you, and to plan ahead to see what you can do in the future.

This cycle of planning, monitoring and evaluation is just as relevant to you as a professional learner as to your students as learners. Be actively in charge of your learning and take appropriate actions. Make your professional development work for you. Of course your professional development programme leaders, trainers and mentors will guide and support you in your learning, but you are at the heart of your own learning experience, not on the receiving end of something that is cast in stone. Those who assist and advise you on your professional development want you and your colleagues to get the best out of the experience, and need your feedback along the way so that if necessary they can adapt and improve what they are devising.

2 Challenge

In principle

Reflection is a constructive process that helps the individual teacher to improve their thinking and practice. It involves regularly asking questions of yourself about your developing ideas and experience, and keeping track of your developing thinking, for example in a reflective journal. Reflection is continuous, rather than a one-off experience. Being honest with yourself means thinking hard, prompting yourself to go beyond your first thoughts about a new experience and to avoid taking for granted your opinions about something to which you are accustomed. Be a critical friend to yourself.

In the Cambridge PDQ Certificate in Teaching and Learning, for example, teachers take a fresh look at the concepts and processes of learning and challenge their own assumptions. They engage with theory and models of effective teaching and learning, and open their minds through observing experienced practitioners, applying new ideas in practice and listening to formative feedback from mentors and colleagues. To evidence in their assessed portfolio how they have learned from this experience, they not only present records of observed practice but also critical analysis showing understanding of how and why practices work and how they can be put into different contexts successfully.

The Cambridge PDQ syllabuses set out key questions to focus professional learning and the portfolio templates prompts to help you. These questions provide a framework for reflection. They are open-ended and will not only stimulate your thinking but lead to lively group discussion. The discipline of asking yourself and others questions such as 'Why?' 'How do we know?' 'What is the evidence?' 'What are the conditions?' leads to thoughtful and intelligent practice.

In practice

Challenge:

- Yourself, as you reflect on an experience, to be more critical in your thinking. For example, rather than simply describing what happened, analyse why it happened and its significance, and what might have happened if conditions had been different.
- Theory – by understanding and analysing the argument, and evaluating the evidence that supports the theory. Don't simply accept a theory as a given fact – be sure that you feel that the ideas make sense and that there is positive value in applying them in practice.
- Convention – the concept of 'best practice(s)' is as good as we know now, on the basis of the body of evidence, for example on the effect size of impact of a particular approach on learning outcomes. By using an approach in an informed way and with a critical eye, you can evaluate the approach relating to your particular situation.

3 Share

In principle

Schools are such busy places, and yet teachers can feel they are working on their own for long periods because of the intensity of their workload as they focus on all that is involved in teaching their students. We know that a crucial part of our students' active learning is the opportunity to collaborate with their peers in order to investigate, create and communicate. Just so with professional learning: teachers learn best through engagement with their peers, in their own school and beyond. Discussion and interaction with colleagues, focused on learning and student outcomes, and carried out in a culture of openness, trust and respect, helps each member of the community of practice in the school clarify and sharpen their understanding and enhance their practice.

This is why the best professional learning programmes incorporate collaborative learning, and pivotal moments are designed into the programme for this to happen frequently over time: formally in guided learning sessions such as workshops and more informally in opportunities such as study group, teach meets and discussion, both face-to-face and online.

In practice

Go beyond expectations!

In the Cambridge PDQ syllabus, each candidate needs to carry out an observation of an experienced practitioner and to be observed formatively themselves by their mentor on a small number of occasions. This is the formal requirement in terms of evidence of practice within the portfolio for the qualification. The expectation is that these are not the only times that teachers will observe and be observed for professional learning purposes (rather than performance appraisal).

However, the more that teachers can observe each other's teaching, the better; sharing of practice leads to advancement of shared knowledge and understanding of aspects of teaching and learning, and development of agreed shared 'best practice'.

So:

- open your classroom door to observation
- share with your closest colleague(s) when you are trying out a fresh approach, for example an idea in this book
- ask them to look for particular aspects in the lesson, especially how students are engaging with the approach – pose an observation question
- reflect with them after the lesson on what you and they have learned from the experience – pose an evaluation question
- go and observe them as they do the same
- after a number of lessons, discuss with your colleagues how you can build on your peer observation with common purpose, for example lesson study
- share with your other colleagues in the school what you are gaining from this collaboration and encourage them to do the same
- always have question(s) to focus observations and focus these question(s) on student outcomes.

Pathways

The short-term effects of professional development are very much centred on teachers' students. For example, the professional learning in a Cambridge PDQ programme should lead directly and quickly to changes in the ways your students learn. All teachers have this at heart – the desire to help their students learn better.

The long-term effects of professional development are more teacher-centric. During their career over, say, 30 years, a teacher may teach many thousand lessons. There are many good reasons for a teacher to keep up-to-date with pedagogy, not least to sustain their enjoyment of what they do.

Each teacher will follow their own career pathway, taking into account many factors. We do work within systems, at school and wider level, involving salary and appointment levels, and professional development can be linked to these as requirement or expectation. However, to a significant extent teachers shape their own career pathway, making decisions along the way. Their pathway is not pre-ordained; there is room for personal choice, opportunity and serendipity. It is for each teacher to judge for themselves how much they wish to venture. A teacher's professional development pathway should reflect and support this.

It is a big decision to embark on an extended programme of professional development, involving a significant commitment of hours of learning and preparation over several months. You need to be as clear as you can be about the immediate and long-term value of such a commitment. Will your programme lead to academic credit as part of a stepped pathway towards Masters level, for example?

Throughout your career, you need to be mindful of the opportunities you have for professional development. Gauge the value of options available at each particular stage in your professional life, both in terms of relevance to your current situation – your students, subject and phase focus, and school – and the future situation(s) of which you are thinking.

14

Understanding the impact of classroom practice on student progress

Lee Davis, Deputy Director for Education, Cambridge International Examinations

Introduction

Throughout this book, you have been encouraged to adopt a more active approach to teaching and learning and to ensure that formative assessment is embedded into your classroom practice. In addition, you have been asked to develop your students as meta-learners, such that they are able to, as the academic Chris Watkins puts it, 'narrate their own learning' and become more reflective and strategic in how they plan, carry out and then review any given learning activity.

A key question remains, however. How will you know that the new strategies and approaches you intend to adopt have made a significant difference to your students' progress and learning? What, in other words, has been the impact and how will you know?

This chapter looks at how you might go about determining this at the classroom level. It deliberately avoids reference to whole-school student tracking systems, because these are not readily available to all schools and all teachers. Instead, it considers what you can do as an individual teacher to make the learning of your students visible – both to you and anyone else who is interested in how they are doing. It does so by introducing the concept of 'effect sizes' and shows how these can be used by teachers to determine not just whether an intervention works or not but, more importantly, *how well* it works. 'Effect size' is a useful way of quantifying or measuring the size of any difference between two groups or data sets. The aim is to place emphasis on the most important aspect of an intervention or change in teaching approach – the **size of the effect** on student outcomes.

Consider the following scenario:

Over the course of a term, a teacher has worked hard with her students on understanding 'what success looks like' for any given task or activity. She has stressed the importance of everyone being clear about the criteria for success, before students embark upon the chosen task and plan their way through it. She has even got to the point where students have been co-authors of the assessment rubrics used, so that they have been fully engaged in the intended outcomes throughout and can articulate what is required before they have even started. The teacher is happy with developments so far, but has it made a difference to student progress? Has learning increased beyond what we would normally expect for an average student over a term anyway?

Here is an extract from the teacher's markbook.

Student	Sept Task	Nov Task
Katya	13	15
Maria	15	20
Joao	17	23
David	20	18
Mushtaq	23	25
Caio	25	38
Cristina	28	42
Tom	30	35
Hema	32	37
Jennifer	35	40

Figure 14.1

Before we start analysing this data, we must note the following:

- The task given in September was at the start of the term – the task in November was towards the end of the term.
- Both tasks assessed similar skills, knowledge and understanding in the student.
- The maximum mark for each was 50.
- The only variable that has changed over the course of the term is the approaches to teaching and learning by the teacher. All other things are equal.

With that in mind, looking at Figure 14.1, what conclusions might you draw as an external observer?

You might be saying something along the lines of: 'Mushtaq and Katya have made some progress, but not very much. Caio and Cristina appear to have done particularly well. David, on the other hand, appears to be going backwards!'

What can you say about the class as a whole?

Calculating effect sizes

What if we were to apply the concept of 'effect sizes' to the class results in Figure 14.1, so that we could make some more definitive statements about the impact of the interventions over the given time period? Remember, we are doing so in order to understand the size of the effect on student outcomes or progress.

Let's start by understanding how it is calculated.

An effect size is found by calculating 'the standardised mean difference between two data sets or groups'. In essence, this means we are looking for the difference between two averages, while taking into the account the spread of values (in this case, marks) around those averages at the same time.

As a formula, and from Figure 14.1, it looks like the following:

$$\text{Effect size} = \frac{\text{average class mark (after intervention)} - \text{average class mark (before intervention)}}{\text{spread (standard deviation of the class)}}$$

In words: the average mark achieved by the class *before* the teacher introduced her intervention strategies is taken away from the average mark achieved by the class *after* the intervention strategies. This is then divided by the standard deviation[1] of the class as a whole.

---

[1] The standard deviation is merely a way of expressing by how much the members of a group (in this case, student marks in the class) differ from the average value (or mark) for the group.

Inserting our data into a spreadsheet helps us calculate the effect size as follows:

	A	B	C
1	Student	September Task	November Task
2	Katya	13	15
3	Maria	15	20
4	Joao	17	23
5	David	20	18
6	Mushtaq	23	25
7	Caio	25	38
8	Cristina	28	42
9	Tom	30	35
10	Hema	32	37
11	Jennifer	35	40
12			
13	Average mark	23.8 = AVERAGE (B2:B11)	29.3 = AVERAGE (C2:C11)
14	Standard deviation	7.5 = STDEV (B2:B11)	10.11 = STDEV (C2:C11)

Figure 14.2

Therefore, the effect size for this class $= \dfrac{29.3 - 23.8}{8.8} = 0.62$

But what does this mean?

Interpreting effect sizes for classroom practice

In pure statistical terms, a 0.62 effect size means that the average student mark **after** the intervention by the teacher, is 0.62 standard deviations above the average student mark **before** the intervention.

We can state this in another way: the post-intervention average mark now exceeds 61% of the student marks previously.

Going further, we can also say that the average student mark, post-intervention, would have placed a student in the top four in the class previously. You can see this visually in Figure 14.2 where 29.3 (the class average after the teacher's interventions) would have been between Cristina's and Tom's marks in the September task.

This is good, isn't it? As a teacher, would you be happy with this progress by the class over the term?

To help understand effect sizes further, and therefore how well or otherwise the teacher has done above, let us look at how they are used in large-scale studies as well as research into educational effectiveness more broadly. We will then turn our attention to what really matters – talking about student learning.

Effect sizes in research

We know from results analyses of the Program for International Student Assessment (PISA) and the Trends in International Mathematics and Science Study (TIMMS) that, across the world, a year's schooling leads to an effect size of 0.4. John Hattie and his team at The University of Melbourne reached similar conclusions when looking at over 900 meta-analyses of classroom and whole-school interventions to improve student learning – 240 million students later, the result was an effect size of 0.4 on average for all these strategies.

What this means, then, is that any teacher achieving an effect size of greater than 0.4 is doing better than expected (than the average) over the course of a year. From our example above, not only are the students making better than expected progress, they are also doing so in just one term.

Here is something else to consider. In England, the distribution of GCSE grades in Maths and English have standard deviations of between 1.5 and 1.8 grades (A★, A, B, C, etc.), so an improvement of one GCSE grade represents an effect size of between 0.5 and 0.7. This means that, in the context of secondary schools, introducing a change in classroom practice of 0.62 (as the teacher achieved above) would result in an improvement of about one GCSE grade for each student in the subject.

Furthermore, for a school in which 50% of students were previously attaining five or more A★–C grades, this percentage (assuming the effect size of 0.62 applied equally across all subjects and all other things being equal) the percentage would rise to 73%.

Now, that's something worth knowing.

What next for your classroom practice? Talking about student learning

Given what we now know about effect sizes, what might be the practical next steps for you as a teacher?

Firstly, try calculating effect sizes for yourself, using marks and scores for your students that are comparable, e.g. student performance on key skills in maths, reading, writing, science practicals, etc. Become familiar with how they are calculated so that you can then start interrogating them 'intelligently'.

Do the results indicate progress was made? If so, how much is attributable to the interventions you have introduced?

Try calculating effect sizes for each individual student, in addition to your class, to make their progress visible too. To help illustrate this, let us return to the comments we were making about the progress of some students in Figure 14.1. We thought Cristina and Caio did very well and we had grave concerns about David. Individual effect sizes for the class of students would help us shed light on this further:

Student	September Task	November task	Individual Effect Size
Katya	13	15	0.22*
Maria	15	20	0.55
Joao	17	23	0.66
David	20	18	-0.22
Mushtaq	23	25	0.22
Caio	25	38	1.43
Cristina	28	42	1.54
Tom	30	35	0.55
Hema	32	37	0.55
Jennifer	35	40	0.55

* The individual effect size for each student above is calculated by taking their September mark away from their November mark and then dividing by the standard deviation for the class – in this case 8.8.

Figure 14.3

If these were your students, what questions would you now ask of yourself, of your students and even of your colleagues, to help you understand why the results are as they are and how learning is best achieved? Remember, an effect size of 0.4 is our benchmark, so who is doing better than that? Who is not making the progress we would expect?

David's situation immediately stands out, doesn't it? A negative effect size implies learning has regressed. So, what has happened, and how will we draw alongside him to find out what the issues are and how best to address them?

Why did Caio and Cristina do so well, considering they were just above average previously? Effect sizes of 1.43 and 1.54 respectively are significantly above the benchmark, so what has changed from their perspective? Perhaps they responded particularly positively to developing assessment rubrics together. Perhaps learning had sometimes been a mystery to them before, but with success criteria now made clear, this obstacle to learning had been removed.

We don't know the answers to these questions, but they would be great to ask, wouldn't they? So go ahead and ask them. Engage in dialogue with your students, and see how their own ability to discuss their learning has changed and developed. This will be as powerful a way as any of discovering whether your new approaches to teaching and learning have had an impact and it ultimately puts data, such as effect sizes, into context.

Concluding remarks

Effect sizes are a very effective means of helping you understand the impact of your classroom practice upon student progress. If you change your teaching strategies in some way, calculating effect sizes, for both the class and each individual student, helps you determine not just *if* learning has improved, but by *how much*.

They are, though, only part of the process. As teachers, we must look at the data carefully and intelligently in order to understand 'why'. Why did some students do better than others? Why did some not make any progress at all? Use effect sizes as a starting point, not the end in itself.

Ensure that you don't do this in isolation – collaborate with others and share this approach with them. What are your colleagues finding in their classes, in their subjects? Are the same students making the same progress across the curriculum? If there are differences, what might account for them?

In answering such questions, we will be in a much better position to determine next steps in the learning process for students. After all, isn't that our primary purpose as teachers?

Acknowledgements, further reading and resources

This chapter has drawn extensively on the influential work of the academics John Hattie and Robert Coe. You are encouraged to look at the following resources to develop your understanding further:

Hattie, J. (2012). *Visible Learning for Teachers – Maximising Impact on Learning*. London and New York: Routledge.

Coe, R. (2002). *It's the Effect Size, Stupid. What effect size is and why it is important.* Paper presented at the Annual Conference of The British Educational Research Association, University of Exeter, England, 12–14 September, 2002. A version of the paper is available online on the University of Leeds website.

The Centre for Evaluation and Monitoring, University of Durham, has produced a very useful effect size calculator (available from their website). Note that it also calculates a confidence interval for any effect size generated. Confidence intervals are useful in helping you understand the margin for error of an effect size you are reporting for your class. These are particularly important when the sample size is small, which will inevitably be the case for most classroom teachers.

15 Recommended reading

The resources in this section can be used to build on your awareness of English as a Second Language teaching and the pedagogical themes in this series.

For a deeper understanding of the Cambridge approach, refer to the Cambridge International Examinations website (www.cie.org.uk/teaching-and-learning) where you will find the following In-depth guides:

Implementing the curriculum with Cambridge; a guide for school leaders.

Developing your school with Cambridge; a guide for school leaders.

Education briefs for a number of topics, such as active learning and bilingual education. Each brief includes information about the challenges and benefits of different approaches to teaching, practical tips, lists of resources.

Getting started with... These are interactive resources to help to explore and develop areas of teaching and learning. They include practical examples, reflective questions, and experiences from teachers and researchers.

For further support around becoming a Cambridge school visit Cambridge-community.org.uk.

Chapter 4

Lewis, M. (1997). *Implementing the Lexical Approach*. Hove, UK: Language Teaching Publications.
Thornbury, S. (2011). *Uncovering Grammar*. Basingstoke, UK: Macmillan.
Underhill, A. (2005). *Sound Foundations*. Basingstoke, UK: Macmillan.

Chapter 5

Richards, J. (2013). *Curriculum Approaches in Language Teaching: Forward, Central, and Backward Design*. London: RELC Journal. Available at Professor Richards' website.
Woodward, T. (2000). *Planning Lessons and Courses*. Cambridge: Cambridge University Press.

Chapter 7

Stahl, R. (1994). *Using 'Think-Time' and 'Wait-Time' Skillfully in the Classroom*. Available online at ERICDigests.org.

Ferlazzo, L. (2014). *Assessing English Language Learners*. Teaching English (British Council/BBC). Available online in Larry Ferlazzo's blog on the TeachingEnglish website.

Roberts, R. (2016). *Feedback – The Most Important Part of Any Exercise?* Teaching English (British Council/BBC). Available online in Rachael Roberts' blog on the TeachingEnglish website.

Chapter 8

Fisher, R. (1998). 'Thinking about thinking: Developing metacognition in children'. *Early Child Development and Care*, 141(1).

Oxford, R. (1990). *Language Learning Strategies*. Belmont, USA: Centage Learning.

Chapter 9

Chadwick, C. (2012). *A Toolkit for Content and Language Teachers*. Cambridge: Cambridge University Press.

Coyle, D. (2010). CLIL (*Content and Language Integrated Learning*). Cambridge: Cambridge University Press.

Harrison, J. (2015). *English Profile in Practice*. Cambridge: Cambridge University Press.

Mehisto, P. (2008). *Uncovering CLIL*. Basingstoke, UK: Macmillan.

Thornbury, S. (1997). *About Language*. Cambridge: Cambridge University Press.

Chapter 10

Alladi, S., Bak, T., Duggirala, V., Surampudi, B., Shailaja, M., Kumar Shukla, A., Ray Chaudhuri, J. and Kaul, S. (2013). *Bilingualism Delays Age at Onset of Dementia, Independent of Education and Immigration Status*. Available online on the Neurology.org website.

Benson, P. and Nunan, D. (2005). *Learners' Stories, Differences and Diversity in Language Learning*. Cambridge: Cambridge University Press.

Pilcher, H. (2004). *Chinese Dyslexics Have Problems of Their Own*. Available online on the Nature.com website.

Chapter 11

Dudeeney, G. (2007). *The Internet and the Language Classroom*. Cambridge: Cambridge University Press.

Stanley, G. (2013). *Language Learning with Technology*. Cambridge: Cambridge University Press.

Chapter 14

Watkins C (2015) *Meta-Learning in Classrooms*. The SAGE Handbook of Learning. Edited by Scott D. and Hargreaves E. London: Sage Publications.

Index